ILLUMINATION

A CONTEMPORARY INTERPRETATION OF SCRIPTURE

JOY BRISBANE

© Copyright 2024 Joy Brisbane

Published in the United States by Hill of Content Publishing

Published in the United Kingdom by Hill of Content Publishing

Published in Australia by Hill of Content Publishing

Published in India by Hill of Content Publishing

Distributed by Etoile International Group. Hong Kong.

hillofcontentpublishing.com

PO Box 24 East Melbourne 8002 Victoria Australia

Cover design: Peta French * *Interior design:* Will Gerard

All rights reserved. No part of this publication may be reproduced, stored in a retrieval system or transmitted in any form by any means without the prior permission of the copyright owner. Enquiries should be made to the publisher. Every effort has been made to ensure that this book is free from error or omissions. However, the Publisher, the Author, the Editor or their respective employees or agents, shall not accept responsibility for injury, loss or damage occasioned to any person acting or refraining from action as a result of material in this book whether or not such injury, loss or damage is in any way due to any negligent act or omission, breach of duty or default on the part of the Publisher, the Author, the Editor, or their respective employees or agents. The Author, the Publisher, the Editor and their respective employees or agents do not accept any responsibility for the actions of any person - actions which are related in any way to information contained in this book.

National Library of Australia Cataloguing-in-Publication data:

Brisbane, Joy,
Illumination

Includes index: ISBN: 978-0-6483443-9-1

CONTENTS

Foreword — vii

1. A Different Voice — 1
2. Background — 8
3. Prince of Kings — 11
4. Number Seven — 16
5. Accountabilities — 21
6. Opening Doors — 25
7. Gems — 29
8. The Beasts — 35
9. The Book — 39
10. Worthy is the Lamb — 43
11. Four Horses — 47
12. The Fifth and Sixth Seals — 56
13. The Seventh Seal — 63
14. Four of Seven Angels — 66
15. Disbelief — 71
16. The Voices — 75
17. The Shadow and the Light — 78
18. Mary — 82
19. The Beasts of Sea and Earth — 85
20. Babylon — 89
21. The Seven Plagues — 92
22. The Scarlet Woman — 98
23. Ancient Wisdom — 101
24. The Bride and Groom — 106
25. The Bottomless Pitt — 111
26. The New Jerusalem — 116
27. The Return of Yeshua — 119

Afterword — 123
Praise for Joy Brisbane — 124
Also by Joy Brisbane — 126

SONG OF GRATITUDE

Dedicated to my Dad,
who unknowingly provided the foundation
for the writing of this book more than half a century ago.

Soft music fills my mind, flows through my body.
Each note takes me deeper into the stillness, the sparseness.
And there you are, Master, patiently waiting for me to find you
In the core energy of love beyond expression.

Through timeless space I drift. No longer the human Self
But pure soul, pure energy sliding through the ether
Into the abyss where shines a pinpoint of light.
This light, this power, far beyond my comprehension
Is the force of all creation.

Rapidly, I am drawn to it, as though some magnetic force in its core
Pulls me, pulls me toward its brilliant, impelling central source.
The pulsating life-giving heartbeat of the collective power of love.
My Master, there you stand, a beacon of light
in the vastness of the void.

FOREWORD

Gregory Landsman
Author of Faith Lifting Prayers

As a child, and even as an adult I have often struggled to understand many parts of the Bible. The book of Revelation was no different. To me these visions of ancient times, proclaiming fire and brimstone, had nothing to do with modern day reality or the challenges I was facing in my life.

I had grown up going to church and my grandmother was a champion of Jesus and his teachings. Every night she would encourage me to sit by the side of the bed and pray, but in truth I had no idea why or what it all meant.

Over many years I was able to heal my relationship with God. I even wrote a book of prayers to capture my journey, yet still, so many of the writings of the Bible remained a mystery. They simply didn't align with my experiences. Which is why I was so deeply moved by Illumination and Joy's interpretations of the book of Revelation.

As I read her interpretation of the Lord's Prayer, I felt emotion well up within me, as decades of misunderstanding the role of religion in my life literally brought tears to my eyes.

All of a sudden, something that I had been saying since I was a child like a mantra with little or no meaning, made sense and felt real and heartfelt for the first time.

Illumination is a transformational book that opens the mind and the heart to the power of love and the healing it can bring to our lives and the lives of others. It takes spiritual seekers on a personal journey that challenges us to find a deeper connection to ourselves and to the Infinite source of all creation; gently asking the reader to let go of what no longer serves them, in order to receive and embrace their full potential and the life they came here to live.

You can't help but be touched by the teachings in Illumination. Joy's profound and relatable wisdom is thought provoking and deeply calming, giving the reader an opportunity to approach life with more compassion, harmony and self love.

While my own experience has shown me that the human body can be fragile, the spirit that lives in it is strong, always offering us hope, guidance, love and peace.

We live in challenging times that everyday ask us to choose… to live our life in darkness or to illuminate what is dark by finding our own light.

Joy Brisbane's words are a powerful reminder to walk our spiritual path with grace and to honour our truth; as everything about life and simply being alive deserves to be celebrated and Illumination helps us do just that.

1

A DIFFERENT VOICE

We all must find the shoes that fit our feet as we walk our path of spiritual enlightenment.

When I heard my dad say, from the pulpit of the church in which he was preaching, "Today our reading comes from the book of Revelation," I knew we were in for a sermon based on awful visions and the need for redemption of my wicked ways. I would inwardly sigh and prepare myself for fearful thoughts.

To the Christian world, the man who gave the visions to his disciple and brother, John in the last book of the Bible, The Revelation, he is known as Jesus. To me he is known as Yeshua. Why? Because Yeshua was Jewish. Jesus was never a Christian. He was born into a Jewish family by Mary. Christianity did not begin until years after his death.

I adhere to no religion, but I am deeply spiritual. When I was twenty-seven years of age, I walked away from my background of Christianity and the dogma and judgements that went with it. Twenty years prior, I had seen a vision in my bedroom of a beautiful spirit woman. Thus began a life-long journey with psychic ability that led to a place of working as a medium. I am also trained in nursing and Lifeline counselling. The more I have seen and worked with the realm of spirit, the more I have understood that religion is a very different thing to spirituality. They can, and often do, go hand in hand. My beautiful mother showed me that such can be the case. But the man-made rules and regulations that religions adopt, and the fear religions use to keep control of the minds and emotions of the people, were never for me.

If, like me, you have found the last book of the Bible somewhat confusing, and rather terrifying in a haunting kind of way, then hopefully what I uncover will allow you to gain a different perspective on what is going on in the pages of this book, written almost two thousand years ago by Yeshua's disciple and brother, John.

As with my previous book, *Creating Heaven on Earth*, [giving a different voice to the sayings of Jesus], I am writing about The Revelation after an encounter with Yeshua. He requested of me to go back, firstly to the gospels, and then to the last book of the Bible, The Revelation, to give a different perspective to what he had said and what he saw.

I began this adventure from a place of apprehension. My young adult revulsion of this book, created through the teachings of my dad and ministers of churches, still held its power over me. This is not a book I would ever have considered writing, but that compelling and strong soul called Yeshua had other ideas. It was probably because of that actual revulsion, and the intrigue I held as to why anyone would want to read it and believe the preachings that came from it, that brought Yeshua to me with the request, "I want you to write a book based on the last book of the Bible; the book of The Revelation." He knew the rebel inside of me would see it through different eyes.

My husband, who was sitting up in bed beside me at the time Yeshua spoke to me, was shocked when I yelled out to Yeshua, "You want me to do what? No way! I can't. I can't go back into that." Poor Allan had no idea who I was talking to, or what it was about. When I told him, I burst into tears, let go, and quietly said, "Your will be done!"

As I began to read each chapter, trying to make sense of it all, I would quietly say, "I have no idea what I am going to write Yeshua. What on earth is this chapter about? Over to you my friend." And to my astonishment I would begin to see through the old-style language to the pictures, the visions Yeshua was presenting to John. The more I moved into the book, the more I began to see, and it was very different to the frightening and controlling messages of the religious leaders in my youth.

I came to realize, the majority of the prophecies Yeshua passed on to John through the visions, were not so much about our personal journey with spirit. They were a forecast on the development of the young Christian faith and its churches; the abuse its followers would have to endure; followed by the fall of the Roman Empire; and finally the raising up of the new Jerusalem within the realm of heaven.

However, I also found many gems of self-realization and illumination of my own inner journey. I found a deeper and more personal relationship with the Master. My in-depth study of a book, that once haunted me with its darkness, has helped me to heal a time of confusion and disenchantment with my very religious father and his perception of what the book of The Revelation meant for him.

Beyond the sometimes dark and mysterious visions that Yeshua apparently imparted to John, hidden in these pages will be some amazing and beautiful moments of awakening to a different and profound voice. A voice which, in the past, was often deliberately portrayed by Christian leaders to be a fearful one - to hold us in a place of obedience and contrition. A controlling power wielded to keep us in servitude and ignorance.

I now enjoy being in my latter seventies, and I have become a little wiser than to simply accept what others wish me to believe. The numbers are falling away from the churches, and it is time for them to ask the question – why? Perhaps it is because these books, written two thousand years ago, appear to bear little relevance to our more advanced technological society. A society that can't even understand some of the stories, and doesn't want to be burdened with ancient teachings that seem to be filled with fear. I ask the question, who reads the Bible now except for devoted Christians? And when was the last time such devout Christians studied the book, The Revelation?

Throughout my life, independence and strength have helped me to maneuver my way through difficult times. I value my independence as others would value gold. Independence and the right to be me, to have my own truth and voice, has helped me to walk a path often strewn with obstacles that threatened to bring me down. Those rough times helped me to find my own deep inner power, a power that can only come from my soul and my desire to remain true to who I am.

Through my journey with the Master and John, I have discovered a truth very different to the one my dad embraced. You may agree with my dad, and find my discoveries foreign, and that is perfectly okay. I am neither interested in agreement nor disagreement, only to give you, the reader, an opportunity to think for yourself and embrace what is right for you. Each of us brings to this world our unique perspectives, a thread in the overall tapestry. We all must find the shoes that fit our feet as we walk our path of spiritual enlightenment.

Remember, as we open the verses of this often-strange book of The Revelation, it was written two thousand years ago and has been interpreted into different languages since that time. A lot can get lost from language to language, and we are relying on the perspective of the translator. I am no expert, and this is not another translation. What I aim to achieve in the writings of this book is to extract the gems as I see them and shift the fear from these rather daunting stories.

I would like to demonstrate how translation through languages can change wording and therefore, our vision of the truth. Let us take the Lord's Prayer as an example. The common use of the Lord's Prayer, translated from Aramaic to Greek to Latin to English reads:

Our Father who art in heaven,
Hallowed be thy name.
Thy kingdom come.
Thy will be done on earth as it is in heaven.
Give us this day our daily bread, and forgive us our trespasses,
As we forgive those who trespass against us,
And lead us not into temptation, but deliver us from evil.
For thine is the kingdom and the power, and the glory, forever and ever.
Amen.

Now let's see what the version looks like, translated back in 2015 from Aramaic directly into English:

Abwûn
Oh Thou, from whom the breath of life comes,

6 | ILLUMINATION

d'bwaschmâja
Who fills all realms of sound, light, and vibration.

Nethkâdasch schmach
May Your light be experienced in my utmost holiest.

Têtê malkuthach:
Your Heavenly Domain approaches.

Nehwê tzevjânach aikâna d'bwaschmâja af b'arha:
Let Your will come true – in the universe just as on earth.

Hawvlân lachma d'sûnkanân jaomâna:
Give us wisdom for our daily need.

Waschboklân chaubên wachtahên aikâna daf chnân schwoken l'chaijabên:
Detach the fetters of faults that bind us (karma) like we let go the guilt of others.

Wela tachlân l'nesjuna:
Let us not be lost in superficial things,

Ela patzân min bischa:
But let us be freed from that what keeps us off from our true purpose.

Metol dilachie malkutha wahaila wateschbuchta l'ahlâm almîn.
From You comes the all-working will, the lively strength to act, the song that beautifies all and renews itself from age to age.

Amên
Sealed in trust, faith, and truth. And so it is.

Wow, what a difference. This reminds me of the Chinese whispers we used to play as children. You take ten people and the person at the beginning of the line whispers a message to the one next to them, and so on down the line. By the time the tenth person has received the message it has completely changed. The Bible has been translated several times through different languages. How much have the visions given to John by Yeshua in The Revelation changed through translation? And have they been deliberately changed through the ages to fit with the Christian churches' control over people, using such visions to place the people into a state of fear and obedience?

There is a wonderful saying by philosopher and psychologist Herbert Spencer (1820-1903] that states:

> *There is a principle*
> *Which is a bar against all information*
> *Which is proof against all arguments*
> *And which cannot fail to keep a man*
> *In everlasting ignorance,*
> *That principle is*
> *Contempt prior to investigation.*

As we delve into the hidden secrets in this last book of the Bible, let it be one of revelation and illumination, as we let go of contempt, and open our hearts and minds to a different investigation into the visions given to us by Yeshua.

BACKGROUND

There are truths that are eternal.

Chapter 1: 1 to 3

1. *"The Revelation of Jesus Christ, which God gave unto him, to shew unto his servants' things, which must shortly come to pass; and he sent and signified it by his angel unto his servant John:"*
2. *"Who bare record of the word of God, and the testimony of Jesus Christ, and of all things that he saw."*
3. *"Blessed is he that readeth, and they that hear the words of this prophecy, and keep those things which are written therein: for the time is at hand."*

A prophecy is an interesting vision of the future. It is simply that – a vision of the future. It is not set in concrete. There are two types of prophecy, the positive and the negative. If a prophecy is of the negative kind, the doomsday kind of prophecy such as Nostradamus had, then it is a wakeup call. It offers the opportunity to change how we approach, or are working with, a certain situation. It says, "If you keep going the way you are, this will be the outcome, and you will have to bear the consequences of your decision making." We are seeing the unfolding of Nostradamus' visions now as we face the changes on our planet due to global warming. We didn't listen! Money making has become far more important than the health of our planet. Here we are then, bearing the consequences of our decision making – fires, floods, famine, and greed.

The other piece to note in the third verse are the words, *"for the time is at hand."* So, keeping in mind this was written about two thousand years ago, what relevance do these writings have now?

At the time, John was writing to the seven churches of Asia Minor, now known as modern Turkey. The churches had been newly established after the death of Yeshua, when Mary [mother of Yeshua] and John had travelled to Ephesus in Turkey. I have been to Ephesus and seen the excavations of the old city. The folks of Turkey are happy to claim the dwelling place of Mary and John.

Mary was to return to Jerusalem at a later date, but shortly after Yeshua's crucifixion, there had been an uprising of the Jews against the Roman rulers. There was a lot of ugly fighting, and the disciples fled to other parts of the known world to escape the turmoil and devastation. It is believed that Mary Magdelene escaped to southern France. Hence, from John's point of view, the prophecies he was recording had relevance for what they were all going through at that time… *for the time is at hand*. I doubt he would have had any thoughts of a future two thousand years hence with those words ringing in his ears.

However, this does not discount the messages that are to be found within the book, The Revelation. Perhaps there are those that only speak to that time of John and Mary, but as we found in the previous book, *Creating Heaven on Earth*, there will be messages that are still relevant today. There are truths that are eternal, and mankind has been a slow learner when it comes to matters of the soul.

3

PRINCE OF KINGS

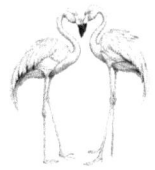

We all have a giant within us that is powerful and eternal.

Chapter 1: 5 to 8

5 *"And from Jesus Christ, who is the faithful witness, and the first begotten of the dead, and the prince of the kings of earth. Unto him that loved us, and washed us from our sins in his own blood."*

6 *"And hath made us kings and priests unto God and his Father; to him be glory and dominion for ever and ever. Amen"*

7 *" Behold he cometh with clouds; and every eye shall see him, and they also which pierced him; and all kindreds of the earth will wail because of him. Even so, Amen."*

8 *"I am Alpha and Omega, the beginning and the ending, saith the Lord, which is, which was, and which is to come, the Almighty."*

There is a lot involved in these few verses. So let's take a look at each verse in turn. But before we do, let us also look at the meaning of the word 'amen'. In our more modern-day use of the word, it has lost some of its significance. Most people see it as meaning, "and so we come to the end." But that is not the actual meaning of 'amen'. Its original meaning is, "it is so, and so it is." Put another way, amen means this is a fact, this is the truth, this is how it is.

I also wish to say that I do not see God as a singular person, a benevolent grandfather type figure sitting on a golden chair somewhere out there in the cosmos. God to me is a huge collective energy far beyond our human comprehension. My personal preference in addressing such energy is more aligned to the words 'Great Spirit', because it encompasses the combined energies of thousands of magnificent beings.

We now know, after two millenniums of scientific research, how incredibly vast our own universe is, and that is not taking into considering all the other known universes. How could one person be accountable for such a massive creation. I believe that such power could potentially be dangerous in the hands of just one being, and the responsibility would be enormous. At the time the Biblical scriptures were written, the peoples knowledge of the universe was a much smaller vision than what we know today. Yeshua's use of the word Father was a deliberate way of helping the people of that time understand that this collective energy was a caring, nurturing, and protective one. He had to present this energy in a way that the people could grasp its intent and feel safe and aligned with it. And so to the verses.

Verse five – *"the first begotten of the dead."* Beget is the present tense meaning - to bring into existence. Begotten is past tense meaning – having brought into existence. So John was saying that Yeshua, the son of Joseph and Mary, was begotten (brought into existence), by the dead. So I can only presume, at the time John wrote this last book of the Bible, Mary had died. Joseph had died before Yeshua had resurfaced in his thirties. And Yeshua was Mary's first child, her first begotten.

Verse five also states – *"and the prince of the kings of earth."* In other words – Yeshua was born a prince in the line of King David and all the kings that followed David. Yeshua was heir to the throne of David. He was an actual prince.

Verse six - *"And hath made us kings and priests unto God and his Father."* Remember, John was addressing the seven newly formed, first time Christian churches in Asia Minor. We tend to see the word church as the name of a building. However, the actual meaning of the word church is a gathering of people. At the time that The Revelation was written, there may not have been actual buildings. To begin, they would most probably have gathered in someone's home. John was writing to the seven groups of people in the seven different towns that were creating the new religion of Christianity. Within these new gatherings, two heads of the church would have been required. The first being the one to administer to the group and guide them at a spiritual level – the priests. The second being the ones to create the new king-dom of Christianity – the kings. King here is not used in the context of earthly royalty, as we know kings. Rather it is used with the meaning of being a leader and protector.

"To him be glory and dominion for ever and ever"… meaning, Yeshua would have dominion over the new church. That from his eternal place in spirit, regardless of the priests and kings at an earth level, Yeshua would reign supreme for all of eternity. And so it is [Amen].

Verse seven - *"Behold he cometh with clouds…"* Why with clouds? Christians have waited a long time for Yeshua's physical return. But would they recognize him as being the Master and prophet if he did return? Or would they think of him as an imposter as the Jews did, and crucified him for his efforts? I feel the hint here is in the word 'clouds'. I don't believe John was talking about a physical return, but rather an ethereal one, as in the clouds. And in this way, he returned a very long time ago. Clouds have been used as a symbol of the realm of spirit for a long time. Within our more modern-day Tarot and oracle card packs, clouds are usually a depiction of spirit. As it was then, so it still is today.

Yeshua was an expert in talking in parables, and using visualizations to make a point. He taught his disciples well in getting a message across to the people by using such language. Whenever my dad spoke about Yeshua returning to Earth, inside my young and immature self I used to scream, but he already has, you just can't see him!

I would never have dared to contradict my dad in matters of the Bible. He made it very clear to me that I had a lot to learn, that he was the one who would teach me, and if I did not believe in what he said, I was a lost soul. My dad had grave concerns for my spiritual welfare. I chose to challenge his beliefs and think for myself. Because of what I was seeing in spirit, I was often in conflict with my dad.

"And every eye shall see him"... That is a big ask. We have a lot more people on this planet than when those words were written. Even then, that was a big statement. So what did John mean? Again, I do not believe the disciple was writing in a physical sense. My personal feeling is this; Yeshua will be remembered, and within our hearts and minds we will hold the vision of him. That vision is not necessarily about his physical form, [although there are plenty of artistic impressions of him around the world], but rather the vision of his love and power to heal.

"And all kindreds of the earth will wail because of him"... Here is a heavy statement if ever I saw one. I am sure the very last thing Yeshua would want for us is to be wailing because of him. His journey here was to bring enlightenment, healing, and a new way forward; not to have people in anguish.

Maybe there is a different way of looking at these words. For me, these words mean that people will *bring* their sorrows, their grief, and their anguish to him with the hope of gaining comfort and healing, *"because of him."* And to this day they still do.

Verse eight – *"I am Alpha and Omega, the beginning and the ending, saith the Lord."* The beginning and the ending of what? Certainly not of the soul, for it is eternal. Yeshua's soul, our souls - they never die. The Alpha is the first letter in the Greek alphabet, the Omega is the last. The Greek language was widely spoken in Yeshua's part of the world at that time, so it is not surprising that he uses these letters to help us understand he is eternal.

Here is where I go with this saying – *"the beginning and the end."* It is rather like numerology. In numerology one is about new beginnings, and nine is about endings. But then along comes ten. You remove the zero off ten – zero being a nothing number and you are back at the beginning again. In other words, Alpha and Omega are part of a never-ending circle. Soul to conception; conception to birth; birth through to old age; and old age through to death, back into spirit with our soul energy. We are born [Alpha], we die [Omega] only to do it all over again through incarnation. So, in truth, we are all the Alpha and Omega. And the last three phrases validates this: *"which is, which was, and which is to come, the Almighty."* Our souls are also 'all-mighty'. And that, I feel, is the whole point of what Yeshua was trying to say.

As human beings we forget how mighty our souls are. We all have a giant within us that is powerful and eternal. That giant can bring incredible love and healing into the world when we let go of being our ego-driven small self, and allow ourselves to stand in the greatest power of all – unconditional love.

4

NUMBER SEVEN

A new beginning...

Chapter 1: 12 to 16

12 'And I turned to see the voice that spake with me. And being turned, I saw seven golden candlesticks';

13 'And in the midst of the seven candlesticks, one unto like the son of man, clothed with a garment down to the foot, and girt about the paps with a golden girdle.'

14 "His head and his hairs were white like wool, as white as snow; and his eyes were as flame of fire;"

15 "And his feet like unto fine brass, as if they burned in a furnace; and his voice as the sound of many waters."

16 "And he had in his right hand seven stars; and out of his mouth went a sharp two-edged sword: and his countenance was as the sun shineth in his strength."

What a vision John had. I know there will be sceptics who feel this is just a fairy tale. Well there are two things I wish to share which allow me to believe in the vision John had. But, before I do, there are another two things to remember about this vision:

- Because it has been translated a number of times, aspects of the vision may have been changed through the interpreter's eyes.
- The Jewish people at that time were very much into working with their psychic gifts. After all, this book is not called 'The Revelation' for no reason. It is all about visions and prophecies. It always baffles me why some Christians find the use of psychic ability so difficult to accept when the man their religion is based on was doing hands on healing, seeing visions, working as a prophet, and using his intuition to know what was going on with those around him. Intuition being one of the six psychic gifts. And still, Yeshua was a learned man, a Rabbi in the Jewish community.

What I wish to share, in support of John's vision, are two incidents that have happened to me, both of which had a major impact upon my life. The first happened when I was seven years of age (there is that number again!). It was evening. I had washed my face and hands, said my prayers, and my mother had just left the room after tucking me up in bed. Suddenly there was a bright light in the room. Standing in the middle of the light was a beautiful woman. She did not say a word. She simply smiled at me. I was not afraid. What I felt coming from her was a lot of warmth and love. I felt protected. Then she faded away. I knew what I had seen was special, yet within me was pure acceptance, as if this was quite a normal and natural thing to happen. I was to find out later, through the reactions of my parents, that this was not normal, and they were afraid of what it would mean for me. I learned quickly not to share my visions. Seventy years later, I am still seeing visions.

The second incident occurred after the death of my husband in 2002. I sold our home, bought land, and built a new home in a completely different area of our state. This was my new beginning, painful as it was as I worked through my grief. One afternoon, sitting in the lounge of my newly built house, I was contemplating my future and if I should begin to use my psychic abilities within the world. From out of nowhere came a booming male voice that stated, "The time is not now!" Now, even for me who was used to psychic phenomena, that voice absolutely shocked me. To this day I have no idea who said it. I know it came from spirit, and that is all I know. John's description of the voice he heard - *and his voice as the sound of many waters* – is very close to what I heard, like a thundering waterfall. And remember, Neale Donald Walsch also had a similar experience. So when I read these few verses of John's visions, I have no hesitation in believing them to be true... even if a little embellished by successive interpreters.

The number seven is a significant number in numerology and at a spiritual level. It is the number for a spiritual quest. It also means perfection, balance, and completeness. It is all about pursuing one's spiritual journey, connecting with our deeper self, and finding unity with the realm of spirit. It begs the question for me, why did the disciples choose seven places to begin their new religion? Coming from the Jewish perspective, which they all were originally, it was perhaps the magical number for the beginnings of their new religion. Numerology has always been important to Jewish people.

Here we find in John's encounter with Yeshua, there were seven candles representing each of the new churches. And in the Master's right hand he held seven stars. Later on we read that the seven stars represented the seven angels, one per church, which was allocated to each group of people to watch over them and protect them so the new religion would be able to flourish.

The vision John had of Yeshua was that of a man – *"one unto like the son of man."* He looked to John exactly as he had looked when here in human form, son of man. The description, *"his eyes were as flame of fire"*, symbolically relates to the intensity of power that shone through Yeshua's eyes. I do not believe they were actually on fire. Nor would his feet have been actually *"like unto fine brass, as if they burned in a furnace."* Again, we have symbolism here to describe how magnificent and strong Yeshua had become; and it may also be a reference to how much his feet had healed after having nails driven through them. And he held in his mouth a *"sharp two-edged sword."* Often the two-edged sword was a metaphor relating to the words of God that could cut out the negative aspects of one's spiritual journey. A double-edged sword can cut both ways and is therefore more powerful. It is also seen as bringing justice to a situation and protection. He was *"girt about the paps with a golden girdle."* Girt – surrounded. In Australia's national anthem we sing 'our land is girt by sea'. Paps – chest or a woman's breasts. So here John sees Yeshua with a golden girdle wrapped around his chest. The girdle, worn in ancient Greece, was seen as representing strength and power. And gold is of course about wealth and the higher power of a king.

When we put all of that information together, we have Yeshua appearing to John in such a way as John would recognize who he was. But in doing so, he was allowing John to know who was going to be boss. In the previous chapter we have the acknowledgement that Yeshua would reign supreme, having dominion over the new church. He stood in the middle of the seven candles that represented each of the new churches, indicating, I will be with you. And in his hand he held the seven stars representing the seven angels he was sending, one to each of the churches. The intensity of his energy can be seen in his eyes and the beautiful light, like the sun, that glowed all around him. And then the golden breast girdle signifying yet again his strength and power, and his position as having dominion over the seven groups of people, but also allowing them to know they would flourish. And lastly, the gold girdle was worn where the heart chakra was placed, signifying his pure and unconditional love and care for them.

Yeshua's reign over Christianity has lasted two thousand years. Christian folk have waited a very long time for his return. Will he come back in physical form? I doubt it, because he is already back, and has been for two thousand years. As a magnificent spirit being, he is far more powerful than he could ever have been if he had returned as a human. It is my belief that the appearance of Yeshua to John in this vision was, in fact, his second coming. And, like many great leaders with a spiritual base, should he return in physical form he is likely to be imprisoned like Nelson Mandela, or shot like Ghandi. Do you think he would want to repeat a horrid death?

5

ACCOUNTABILITIES

The inner journey of self-discovery.

As I read the second chapter of this book, The Revelation, I found myself being challenged by some of the language in it. My connection to Yeshua, over many years, and my impressions of him do not line up with what has been written. I know him to be a strong personality, who can be quite demanding, [he had to have a strong and powerful personality to go through what he did in his human life], but I have never seen him as judgmental or handing out punishment, as this version of his conversation with John would indicate.

This was not a chapter I knew from my dad's influence. It was not one from which he preached a sermon as far as I can remember. After reading the full chapter I sat, eyes closed, thinking about my connection to Yeshua and asking the question, "Have I been living with an illusion of who I want him to be, rather than with reality?" Something inside of me yelled – NO! Then, out loud I said, "I don't believe what I am reading. I just don't believe it. This is not who you are. This is a human beings interpretation that is inaccurate; an interpretation that was influenced by the interpreter's own opinions. But how can I say for sure that what I believe is correct?" Suddenly, I felt a flow of energy move through my body. With that energy came warmth and incredible love. My heart filled with his warmth and love to the point of tears from the impact it was having on me. I had my answer. Yeshua showed me, in the best way he knew how, that the truth of what he had said to John had been cancelled because of the interference of translation and the beliefs of the interpreters.

I can only bring to you my truth in what I see in this second chapter. I leave it with you to make a choice as to what feels right for you. Rather than me copying all of the verses, I suggest you find a copy of it online: St James version, The Revelation, second and third chapters. However, here is a summary of what is happening in this piece of writing from John - as I see it.

Yeshua is speaking to him about the seven angelic beings that were sent to each church to help them establish the new religion. Each angel took on the form of a human being. Once here, all except one forgot from whence they had come, and these six fell into the traps of human existence. Here are the ways in which these angels took on their human form.

- Ephesus – that angel worked hard and developed patience for even the most trying of the flock. However, he deserted his first love.
- Smyrna – this angel also worked hard, and lived in poverty with many problems in his life. However, he was told he would be thrown into prison for being Yeshua's supporter, and there he would die.
- Pergamos – this angel was faithful in his beliefs, but

he mixed with people of other beliefs and lowered himself to fornication [sexual delight].
- Thyatira – he had patience and care for the people, and was charitable in his service to them. He helped those who were of the lesser society to be raised up to higher levels of attainment. But he was friends with a woman called Jezebel who claimed to be a prophetess. She seduced people into fornication, and to eat food that was sacrificed to idols.
- Sardis – this angel was living as a human, but was dead to his inner spiritual journey. He was directed to remember his angelic origins, and to take off the clothes of his human self and put on the white clothes of his inheritance of purity.
- Philadelphia – the one angel that remembered who he was. To this angel, who had deep inner strength, people would come and worship at his feet. Yeshua left a message for him saying that he was well loved.

What is all of this telling us? We all have beautiful souls, within which is housed our magnificent spirit. When we pass through the flimsy curtain of death back into spirit, we remember who we truly are. When we are born into this world, our memory of where we have come from is lost to us. As little babies we may still hold fragments of memory, but the more we integrate into our human existence, the more we forget our origins. Life brings us many challenges, and often we mess things up. But this world is university training for the soul. Here we learn strength, courage, patience, persistence, and service to our fellow people. It is our project, having forgotten our origins, to remember again, and come into acceptance of our divinity, our heritage, our birth right to be the gorgeous and magical being we are.

Like these seven angelic beings, we and only we, are accountable for the choices we have made, for the paths we have chosen to walk, and for our attitudes toward self and others. We always have the choice to live in our lesser ego-driven small self, or to search deeply and find our greatness, our giant within, our eternal spirit. As we take the inner journey of self-discovery, we too will find what the angel of Philadelphia found – the deep and abiding love for self and for all people. And we will know and feel the love coming to us from Great Spirit.

And so it is, and so it will be.

OPENING DOORS

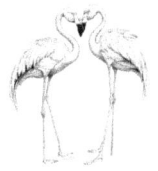

Opening ourselves up to the wonder and power of our inner giant – our soul.

Chapter 3: 20 and 21

20 *"Behold, I stand at the door, and knock: if any man hear my voice, and open the door, I will come in to him, and I will sup with him, and he with me."*

21 *"To him that overcometh will I grant to sit with me in my throne, even as I also overcame, and am set down with my Father in his throne."*

"I stand at the door and knock..." Which door? Remembering that Yeshua is now fully back in spirit, having left this realm of Earth after his crucifixion. I think it is safe to say it can't be the door of a physical building. I presume it is the door to our heart, mind, and soul. Note he says, *I will come in to him*, not I will enter his home. Put differently, if a person opens the door of their heart, mind, and soul to me, I will become one with that person.

"I will sup with him, and he with me." The word sup means to drink. I will share a drink with this person, and they will drink with me. Again this cannot mean at a physical level, which begs the question, to which kind of drink is the Master referring? The common drink at that time would be either water or wine.

- Water – the vital element to our existence. We cannot live without it.
- Wine – that which celebrates our life.

Perhaps he meant both water and wine; the life-giving force and the celebration of our lives. Either way, the message Yeshua was conveying was one of sharing, caring, and unity of spirit. I will nourish this person and, in so doing, I will be nourished.

Our connection with our guides in spirit, [Yeshua being one of many], is never a one-way street. What we do on their behalf in helping others, they will do for us. Our welfare is uppermost in their connection to us. It is a lot more difficult for those in spirit to do their work here if we are not available to them. We need them, and they need us. It may not always look like they have our best interest at heart. Often we blame them for what we have actually created for ourselves through our negative responses to life. But sometimes, that which seems hard brings with it many gifts. If we allow ourselves to look beyond the pain and distress, we will see how healing is happening at a different and deeper level. Our mental, emotional, and soul growth is not always easy, but it is an ongoing process we cannot avoid. If we don't do it in this lifetime, then we will start all over again in our next life – wherever that is.

Extraordinary beings like Yeshua can only 'sup with us' if we allow ourselves to open the door to our hearts and let them in. If the door is not open, they will not enter.

"To him that overcometh will I grant to sit with me in my throne." Yeshua does not say – 'on my throne." He says – 'in my throne'. So what is the true meaning of the word - throne? The use of the word throne is an interesting metaphor the Master chose. This word originated in the Greek language meaning:

- Seat or chair.
- Support – which then became the support of the Heavens, or axis mundi – the meeting of Heaven and Earth – the connectedness – the oneness – and the support of Heaven for Earth.
- Which then became the seat or place of power.

I don't believe that Yeshua was talking about a regal/royal throne. That is our interpretation from this period of time, the throne of royalty and human power. Throne meant something quite different in his time. To sit with Yeshua *in* his throne was to be one with him, to enjoy the power of love and his leadership, to be connected with him and enjoy his everlasting support. And we can only reach that place if we work toward overcoming the smallness of the mind's ego, and opening ourselves up to the wonder and power of our inner giant – our soul.

A small but significant comment coming from the Master was – *"even as I also overcame."* All too often we forget that he was a human being. All the challenges of human existence was present for him, both in his outer world and within himself. He too had to overcome the ego-driven mind and find the spirit within him. I have often said, I believe that Yeshua's human life was just as important as his divine life. Without being fully human, how could he possibly be aware of the challenges we go through? Through his humanity he found his divinity. Through being a man he found compassion, understanding, wisdom, strength, and courage. And so can we if we choose.

"And am set down with my Father in his throne..." Here we have the word 'in' again. Not 'on' his throne. I always question the use of Father when it comes to Yeshua. Does he mean Great Spirit, or does he mean Joseph? I know my dad would say God. But for me it could mean either or both. After all, when I die and move through that fine curtain back into spirit, my earth father will be there, and I will no doubt sup with him in celebration of my return home. And if, as those of a spiritual nature believe, we all become one, already are one, then it makes sense to me that what Yeshua was saying was:

I and my earth father, Joseph, and my heavenly Father, Great Spirit, have become one. I am the axis mundi – the connection and stabilizing energy between heaven and Earth. I sit in the throne - in the power of my soul - with them.

7

GEMS

*Love, healing, nurturing, wholeness, and peace.
We are shown what we need to know for the greater
good of all.*

Chapter 4: 1 to 4

1 "*After this I looked, and behold, a door was opened in heaven: and the first voice which I heard was as it were a trumpet talking with me; which said, Come up hither, and I will shew thee things which must be hereafter.*"

2 " *And immediately I was in the spirit: and, behold, a throne was set in heaven, and one sat on the throne,*"

3 "*And he that was sat was to look upon like a jasper and a sardine stone: and there was a rainbow around the throne, in sight like unto an emerald.* "

4 "*And round about the throne were four and twenty seats: and upon the seats I saw four and twenty elders, sitting, clothed in white raiment: and they had on their heads crowns of gold.*"

What an amazing vision, and one that needs to be unpacked. Before doing so, as a medium and in my own personal experiences with spirit, I can tell you I have gone before what I call the sacred council of twelve many times. Here, in the beginning of chapter four, we have a sacred council of twenty-four. My experience may help to make sense of these four verses.

For centuries, my sacred council of twelve have been helping me on my journey of being unafraid to stand in my chosen place, to be their voice to this planet of Earth. As with many folks, Earth is not my home planet. I have visited here through many lifetimes, learning my lessons so my soul may advance to higher levels – as we all do. But home is somewhere else in this cosmos. I am not alone in saying that there have been times when I have glimpsed my home and felt homesick; wanting to return to the people with whom I feel as one. I believe many mediums go through this process of learning to remain here to achieve what we put our hands up to do, knowing this place is not home to us.

John writes, *"Come up hither, and I will shew thee things which must be hereafter,"* that is exactly the experience of a medium. We not only connect in with spirit, but we also go into spirit in our minds and hearts, losing contact with our human self, and - as is written here - we are shown what we need to know for the greater good of all. Mediums are not a new concept. There is nothing new about the so-called new age. It is all ancient. What is new is that religion is beginning to lose its grip on our free will and free thinking. Yeshua was a medium.

Within my sacred council of twelve there is one who is the spokesperson for the other eleven. He is the commander of the team. The team is made up of both feminine and masculine energy and those that are androgynous. I call him

Father Zu. He has the air of authority like a king. When Yeshua speaks of his father 'who art in heaven', he may also be referring to his leader of his sacred council of twenty-four. Perhaps the more advanced a soul we are, the more souls we need on our sacred council to supervise our journey. One thing is certain. The beings in these sacred councils are extremely highly evolved souls. My council is probably supervising hundreds of humans such as myself. I am sure there are many sacred councils supervising what is happening throughout the cosmos.

"After this I looked, and behold, a door was opened in heaven." Another way of saying 'door' is to speak of a portal. Such portals I often see. It is rather like that gap in the clouds that allows the beams of light to flow through. There is nothing new about portals. Science fiction authors write about them. Thousands of people throughout time have experienced portals. They are what John says – doorways into other realms.

"And the first voice which I heard was as it were a trumpet talking with me." In chapter three I have referred to the sound of a physical voice from spirit. It can be big and loud.

In verse two we read – *"And immediately I was in the spirit: and, behold, a throne was set in heaven, and one sat on the throne."* Remembering that the word 'throne' has a different connotation to how we perceive a throne, the one who sat in that seat of divine power, like Father Zu, would have been the leader of the council of twenty-four.

"And he that was sat was to look upon like a jasper and a sardine stone." When I read sardine stone, I immediately had a vision of grey and small fish. I thought, surely that cannot be right. Research tells me that sardine stone is what we now know as ruby, and jasper is what we know as diamond. The jasper we know is a very different stone to

the one John was referring to. How words change through the centuries.

The people of that time knew the qualities of gemstones. Apart from the appearance of wealth, castles were adorned with gemstones. Why? Because of the encased energy within them derived through millions of years of compression in the womb of Earth. The ancient ones understood the significance of the power of gemstones. The royal crown of England has many such stones around its rim and at the core center of the crown, and each gem signifies something about the power granted to the one who wears it.

What John is saying here – the leader of the council of twenty-four - he had an energy field around him of vibrant glowing red, and a light like diamonds shining around him and through him.

We all have energy fields. Our energy field moves at a certain vibrational rate according to our thoughts and feelings. It gives off colours that reveal our state of being. The colours change depending on what mood we are in and if our thoughts are negative or positive. John then goes on to say that around this powerful being was an arching rainbow, the colour of an emerald.

Let me examine what each of these gems and their colours mean. It will help us to understand what gorgeous power and beauty this being has.

- Ruby [sardine] – the stone of love. [Sometimes thought of as the spilt blood of Yeshua]. Ruby is also about nurturing, obtaining knowledge, and wealth in its many forms. Wealth and abundance are not only about the gathering of money and material possessions. One can have a wealth of knowledge

and wisdom – which in the case of this being is highly appropriate.
- Diamond [jasper] – another stone of love. Diamond is also about durability – the hardest gem we have – elegance, supreme nurturing, support in times of stress; and aids in creating wholeness and tranquility.
- Emerald – the stone of the heart chakra, and yet another stone of love. It is a stone for healing and nurturing the heart. It brings balance to emotions and matters of the heart. Emeralds bring vitality to our soul and enhance our spiritual growth.

There are, of course, other qualities to these three gemstones, but in relation to this being of divine power, wow, what a line-up of love, healing, nurturing, wholeness, and peace. All a reflection of who Yeshua was, and what he came to this Earth realm to teach.

"And upon the seats I saw four and twenty elders, sitting, clothed in white raiment: and they had on their heads crowns of gold." If we were to take this literally from our present-day perspective, we would have to say here are twenty-four kings and queens. But, again, this is a metaphor relating to the power these beings have. So, let us look to see what gold means.

- Honour
- Wealth in all of its forms
- Happiness and amplifies positive feelings
- Stability and the release of tension and trauma
- Embodiment of divine qualities
- Enabling healing

They were clothed in white garments. White is the colour of purity, wholeness, light ,[which embodies all colour], and completeness. These twenty-four souls are of a high standing for they have come into their wholeness. They have completed their journeys of learning and become beings of light in service and guidance to those who are still on their path to wholeness.

We all have our sacred council beings who watch our progress. Most folk are unaware of them, but that does not negate their presence. From what I experience, my main guides are with me all of the time. However, occasionally, when it is required, my main guide takes me before the sacred council of twelve. There is always a reason, and usually it is about the next major step I am required to take on my chosen journey toward completeness. Each time it happens I see all twelve dressed in white. For most of them I cannot see who they are. Always it is he who I call Father Zu who speaks with me... *"as it were a trumpet talking with me."*

We all have far more help available to us within spirit than we can possibly know. Their support is limited because they cannot cross the boundary of our free will. To know the fullness of that support requires us to open our hearts and minds to the possibilities, then to trust that, regardless of what seems apparent, these beings have our souls best interest at heart.

The more I let go of needing to control – the more control I am given. Such is the paradox of life. And behind every leg of this journey I am on, there are magnificent beings supporting every step I take.

If you like... let go and let God.

8

THE BEASTS

Four elements of Earth and our inter-connectedness with Earth
The cleansing and purity of power.

Chapter 4: 5-7

5 *"And out of the throne proceeded lightnings, and thunderings and voices: and there were seven lamps of fire burning, before the throne, which are the seven Spirits of God."*

6 *"And before the throne there was a sea of glass like unto crystal: and in the midst of the throne, and around about the throne, were four beasts full of eyes before and behind."*

7 *"And the first beast was like a lion, and the second beast like a calf, and the third beast had a face as a man, and the fourth beast was like a flying eagle."*

Visions are like dreams; they need interpretation. Visions occur in the same part of the brain where dreams occur and operate on similar brain waves. Mostly they are metaphors or symbols. Usually, we wake from our dreams feeling confused, wondering what they were all about, what the dream was trying to tell us. And so it is with visions. Cup of coffee in hand, it is time for some lateral thinking - as we do with our dreams.

"And there were seven lamps of fire burning, before the throne, which are the seven Spirits of God." Remembering that a throne is not necessarily an ornate chair, but rather is a place of leadership and power, or axis mundi – the meeting of Heaven and Earth – the connectedness – the oneness – and the support of Heaven for Earth, a place where highly evolved souls gather together under the leadership of an even more powerful being. Here were seven lamps burning. For me, these seven lamps represented the first seven churches of the new religion. To John, the new churches would have seemed like amazing lights burning out of a torrid and dark past. Each one representing the Spirits of God. Another way of saying this could be, each lamp represented the seven angelic beings appointed to each church from the realm of Great Spirit.

"And before the throne there was a sea of glass like unto crystal." Crystals, as I have mentioned before, were used for purposes of healing and power. Our modern use of crystals is a remembering of the past, and a re-igniting of their abilities to bring the energy within them into useful purpose. For those who doubt the use of crystals, remember you have clear quartz crystal in your cars, your watches, and your computers to enhance the energy that drives them. From John's description of this vision, to look like a sea of glass that sparkles like a crystal, it may well have been the image of clear quarts. My feelings about this *"sea of glass like crystal"* is a reference related to cleansing and purity of power. Perhaps like the still water of a large lake?

"And in the midst of the throne, and around about the throne." Here again we have 'in' when speaking about the throne. In

the midst – not simply on or around – but in the midst of the throne and around it. Again, the inference of the throne is not about an ornate chair but a place of power.

"Were four beasts full of eyes before and behind. And the first beast was like a lion, and the second beast like a calf, and the third beast had a face as a man, and the fourth beast was like a flying eagle." There is a variety of opinions as to the symbology of these four beasts, and maybe each opinion is a fragment of the whole. For some they represent the four chosen gospels, [there were other gospels from other disciples and Mary Magdalene that were not included in the New Testament. If they had been, we may have had a very different view of the stories within the New Testament]:

- Matthew – man
- Mark – lion
- Luke – calf [often referred to elsewhere in the Bible as ox]
- John – eagle

Others see them as representing the four elements of Earth and our inter-connectedness with Earth:

- Man – fire – passion and driving force – Matthew
- Lion – earth – strength, fearlessness, stability – Mark
- Calf [ox] – water – another name for ox can be water buffalo – determination, hardworking, durability – Luke
- Eagle – air – protection [sheltering under the wings], all seeing, rising to greater heights, connection between heaven and Earth. Eagle is often seen as a shaman's totem for these reasons – John

Going by the visions John was having, there is certainly the element of shamanism in him. And remembering that these disciples started off within the Jewish faith, only later becoming Christians, psychic ability was common and accepted by them. After all, the Master himself was fully aware of his psychic gifts as a prophet and healer. And the eyes *before and behind* them simply mean not missing anything, seeing it all, being very observant.

And for others the four beasts represent four angelic beings, [or cherubim], all of whom would also have the qualities suggested above.

What is this vision telling us? It is simple. From the throne of power within spirit all of these qualities were available to the new churches, and are still available to us as individuals.

The stories within this last book of the Bible can appear frightening, and all too often throughout the last two millennium, leaders of the Christian faith have used this book to create fear in the hearts of people, to manipulate them into being who those leaders want the people to be. But when we remove the element of fear, and see these visions for their true worth, then there is much beauty to be found in these ancient writings of John.

THE BOOK

The book held guidance not judgement.

Chapter 5: 1-5

1 *"And I saw in the right hand of him that sat on the throne a book written within and on the backside, sealed with seven seals."*

2 *"And I saw a strong angel proclaiming with a loud voice, who is worthy to open the book, and to loose the seals thereof?"*

3 *"And no man in heaven, nor in earth, neither under the earth, was able to open the book, neither to look thereon."*

4 *" And I wept much, because no man was found worthy to open and to read the book, neither to look thereon."*

5 *"And one of the elders saith unto me, Weep not: behold the Lion of the tribe of Juda, the root of David, hath prevailed to open the book, and to loose the seven seals thereof."*

No one knows what the book held within its pages. John never enlightens the reader as to its contents. Some believe it was a scroll that held the judgement of God on sin and wickedness. Was it not Yeshua who said in Matthew 7: verse

1, "judge not that ye be not judged?" I have to question the assumption of religious leaders in believing the book was full of judgements. If that Master did not believe in the act of judgement, why would he open a book on judgement?

Fear is the product of an ego-driven mind. Love is the product of heart, soul and spirit. Negative judgement, the threat of eternity in hell, the damning of a person, they arise from a base of fear. Yeshua and Great Spirit are egoless. They are of love. Therefore, the interpretations of John's visions that speak of judgement and hell, installing fear into peoples' hearts, have to be of man's making.

In my previous book, *Creating Heaven on Earth*, I have written a chapter called *What is Sin?* Within it is a simple Jewish explanation of how they saw sin - Hata [sin] means – to go astray. It does not have the same force of negative energy to it that Christians have since placed on the word. We have all gone astray at some stage in our life, but that does not mean we are bad people. It simply means we have lost sight of our path.

It amazes me that people to this day see this body of work by John as the absolute truth. Surely some healthy questioning needs to take place? Why?

- The wording has been changed through the interpretation of four languages.
- These are visions, and the meaning of a vision can change according to how the metaphors and symbolism are seen.
- John was born into a Jewish family. Therefore, his understanding of his visions will be influenced by his religious past and cultural upbringing of that time.

What were the seven seals? The common belief within the Chrisian faith, they were the seals of the seven spirits [angels] of God. As the seven lamps [previous chapter] represented the seven new churches shining their light into the world, so I feel that these seven seals are a representation of those churches – remembering that right at the very beginning, John states that these visions and writings were for the seven new churches in what is now Turkey. As each seal is opened, there is a message for each of the churches. My personal belief, the book held guidance not judgement, to help the leaders of the seven new churches to stay on the right path... so they would not go astray [Hata].

"And no man in heaven, nor in earth, neither under the earth, was able to open the book, neither to look thereon." What is meant by *under the earth*? Those who have died, who are buried. In other words, those who have returned to spirit – otherwise they would not be able to attempt to open the book. Such was the sacredness of what the book contained, only the one who had moved away from the influence of the ego-driven self, who was fully in the pureness of their spirit, was able to open the book and allow John to pass on to the churches the messages contained within the book. These messages contained in the next couple of chapters came in the form of visions – not in the written word.

"Behold the Lion of the tribe of Juda, the root of David, hath prevailed to open the book, and to loose the seven seals thereof." [Wax seals were still used to close the envelopes of letters until adhesive was introduced in 1830]. Yeshua was seen as the Lion of Juda. Why the lion? The king of beasts bringing strength, fearlessness, and stability. The root of David simply means he was born into the line of David and therefore was heir to the throne of David. Yeshua was a prince. The words – the Prince of Peace, and, unto us a king is born – were a fact. As stated in *Creating Heaven on Earth*, Yeshua's crucifixion

was a political move by the leaders of the Jewish community to silence his voice and to bring him down to the level of murderers and thieves. He was a rebel, and the Jewish leaders did not want someone on the throne who would challenge what they wanted. A big mistake on their behalf. In crucifying Yeshua they turned him into a hero and martyr. That which they feared – they created.

And that is a message for us all. What we fear we create. What we believe to be true – becomes our reality.

It makes sense that Yeshua would be the one to deliver that guidance. This new religion was created from his teachings and wisdom. His disciples had been instructed by him, when he was still alive, to go out into the world and teach what Yeshua had taught them.

John, in the next couple of chapters, delivers those messages in a rather dramatic way.

WORTHY IS THE LAMB

There are many who have brought love and hope into our world.

Chapter 5: 6-10

6. " And I beheld, and, lo, in the midst of the throne and of the four beasts, and in the midst of the elders, stood a Lamb as it had been slain, having seven horns, and seven eyes, which are the seven Spirits of God sent forth into all the earth."

7. "And he came and took the book out of the right hand of him that sat upon the throne."

8. "And when he had taken the book, the four beasts and four and twenty elders fell down before the Lamb, having everyone of them harps, and golden vials full of odours, which are the prayers of saints."

9. " And they sung a new song saying, Thou art worthy to take the book, and to open the seals thereof: for thou wast slain and hath redeemed us to God by they blood out of every kindred, and tongue, and people, and nation;"

10. And hast made us unto our God, kings and priests; and we shall reign on the earth.

In verse six, the reference to *"a lamb as it had been slain"*, is a reference to Yeshua appearing as he had appeared when crucified, and after his crucifixion. Lambs were used as a sacrifice on the altars of places of worship. Yeshua was seen, by those who loved him, as the sacrificial lamb. The elders, being the members of his sacred council. The word elders is a reference to beings of wisdom and knowledge. Having seven horns – the horns of cattle and sheep were used like a trumpet, to summon the people together. One horn per church to bring the people together. And, of course, again the eyes to observe what is happening as the new churches grow and develop. The last sentence is again a reference to the seven angels – *"which are the seven Spirits of God sent forth into all of the earth."*

Verse seven is a reference to Yeshua taking the book from the leader of the council of twenty-four. Also, in accepting the book, he accepted the responsibility for the welfare and workings of the seven churches.

And what a scene we have in verse eight. As Yeshua received the book, this was a time of celebration. By allowing himself to receive the book, he had made a commitment to be the head of the new seven churches. From the realm of Great Spirit, he would communicate with the seven angels, who had been sent to the churches in human form, and he was accepting the role of being the ruler of the new religion.

It is interesting to make reference to the seven vials that contained *odours*, now known as essential oils. If you remember, at his birth Yeshua was given frankincense and myrrh by the three kings. When he died his body was embalmed with those same oils by the women he loved.

Essential oils have been used for centuries because of their healing properties.

Verse nine alludes to the idea that Yeshua was not only present for his Jewish tribes, but that he came to share with all people on earth his wisdom, knowledge, and healing abilities.

In Verse ten, the statement of being made kings and priests is in reference to the leadership, physical and spiritual, of those appointed to bring the seven churches into existence. And reign on the earth they did, but not always with loving intent.

I sometimes wonder how Yeshua would feel today, knowing how many people have died at the hands of Christians; how wars have been fought under the banner of Christianity; how many people were persecuted for not doing what those kings and priests wanted them to do; how the manipulation of people's minds and hearts have imprisoned their lives.

There are many who have brought love and hope into our world through their Christian faith. To this day his wisdom and knowledge are still important to us, hence my book Creating Heaven on Earth and this book, Illumination. And people are still calling on Yeshua's spirit to help them to heal. But dark and the light will always exist in opposite extremes when human nature, the ego, steps in to override the beauty of the divine nature of Great Spirit. Christianity does not rule as it once did; although there are still threads of that rule remaining in places such as the Vatican and other fundamentalist sects of Christianity. More and more, people are searching for a spiritual path that fits for them, without being drawn in to the dogma of any religion.

Yeshua's new church was meant to bring love, peace, and healing to the people. A new way forward, away from the brutality of what was happening within the Jewish community of that time. But even he could not control the gift of free will mankind was given. That free will, held within the clutches of an ego-driven mind, has brought about the dark side of all religions. The kings and priests became a power unto themselves, losing their deeper connection and journey with spirit.

11

FOUR HORSES

Darkness cannot exist when the pure white light of divine love is present.

I found chapter six to be somewhat confusing. Reading it again after many years of being absent from the Bible, it seemed to me to go against everything that divine love, Yeshua the healer represents, and my understanding of what it means to be in service to humanity. It challenged me considerably to try and understand what the truth really was in these verses. Perhaps the rebellious child within me, the child that feared my dad's voice and his interpretation of the book of Revelation, wanted to once again hide under the safety of her blankets and close her mind to the awful visions.

As Yeshua opened each of the first four seals of seven, his vision, to which John was a witness, was of a horse and its rider. Each seal produced a different coloured horse; each horse and rider with a purpose.

As I sat with the verses, I was reminded of Nostradamus and the visions he saw for the future of our planet and its inhabitants. I began to see how closely aligned they were, and how these visions were a representation of how humanity, with its ego driven sense of power, would unfold as the centuries passed through time. And as I look at what is currently happening in our world, I can see the correlation with these prophecies; for that is what chapter six is all about, a vision into the future of mankind and our endless battle with the negative side of the ego.

Before we move into examining what the messages were trying to convey, let us take a look as to how horses have served us. Prior to the invention of machines bringing us many types of transport, horses were core to daily life. They:

- Carried us on their backs to go from point A to point B; into war; carrying the wounded back to where they could get help; for sporting activities; to work with cattle and sheep; riding into mountainous terrain to rescue people.
- And then there were the pack horses, carrying the heavy loads that men were not strong enough to carry.
- They pulled carts, ploughs, carriages and chained logs felled for wood mills.
- They walked round and around in a circle to grind grain for our sustenance.
- They pulled our first trains and trams.

No doubt you could list many more gifts of service that they gave to us. With loyalty, horses gave us their strength, speed, endurance, companionship, wisdom, and protection. So it is not surprising to me that a horse, as opposed to the camel or donkey, which were other modes of transport at that time, was the chosen animal for Yeshua's visions as he broke each of the seals. For these were the qualities each of us would need as we moved through the centuries to come – strength, endurance, wisdom, companionship, and protection.

These horses are often referred to as the four horses of the apocalypse, inferring a particular time of great upheaval, and perhaps, as some people believe, the ending of our existence on this planet. But there is no time boundary indicated in these writings. When I look back through history, and at where we are now, these prophecies have been present with us for two thousand years. For all of that time we have been fulfilling these prophecies. Both Nostradamus and Yeshua sent out the warning. Have we listened? No! We are still a warring planet. Climate change is allowing us to see how little we have cared for our planet. Our ego driven hunger for ownership and power and to be singularly right, has not abated. We are still allowing greedy and aggressive rulers to create the apocalypse we have been in for the past two millennia. And so to the verses.

Verses 1 and 2:

1 "And I saw [John] when the Lamb [Yeshua] opened one of the seals, and I heard, as it were the noise of thunder, one of the four beasts saying, Come and see,"

2 "And I saw, and behold a white horse, and he that sat on him had a bow; and a crown was given unto him; and he went forth conquering and to conquer."

[The four beasts – chapter 7]

One might ask, why a white horse? What is so special about a white horse? Obviously the rider was someone of importance to have a crown. White depicts purity, and from a Christian point of view, righteousness. Some believe the rider to be Yeshua as a spirit riding into his kingdom, his new church, with a bow to conquer the negative power of mankind's inner darkness. There is only one way to conquer darkness and that is with light. This is possibly another reason why the horse was white. Darkness cannot exist when the pure white light of divine love is present.

Verses 3 and 4

3 *"And when he had opened the second seal, I heard the second beast say, Come and see,"*

4 *"And there went out another horse that was red; and power was given to him that sat thereon to take peace from the earth, and that they should kill one another; and there was given unto him a great sword."*

A red horse, the colour of passion. If you are a person who works with the colours of our chakras, then red is the colour of the base chakra, the one that grounds us and brings us into connection with Mother Earth. The sword is seen as the instrument of truth, cutting out that which is not real and is harmful. Another way of saying *"to take peace from the earth"* would be to see complacency removed; to shake things up a bit and make the people of earth take a good look at what they are doing.

"And that they should kill one another," I do not believe was the rider's purpose, which goes against all the teachings of the Master, but rather that this is what needed to be stopped. Remembering these words may look very different in the original script. If I were to reword these two verses for myself, it would look like this:

Yeshua, full of the fire of passion, and wielding the sword of truth, rode out to shake us from our complacency, to make us look at how we are treating each other with our warring egos, and to bring us back into the awareness of what is true and real.

Verses 5 and 6:

5 "And when he had opened the third seal, I heard the third beast say, Come and see. And I beheld, and lo a black horse; and he that sat on him had a pair of balances in his hand."
6" And I heard a voice in the midst of the four beasts say, A measure of wheat for a penny, and three measures of barley for a penny; and see thou hurt not the oil and the wine."

From my research, the black horse is widely accepted to mean famine. Mostly the reference is to physical famine due to the appearance of the scales and the measurement of grain within the prophecy. When it comes to floods, fire, and famine, food is in short supply and as a result the prices go up. Sound familiar? We are seeing this played out now. The cost of living has risen considerably due to these influences, and the greed of big business. Remembering the distance in time, our planet has seen many famines. Again, the apocalypse seems to be not one massive disaster but many thousands of years of existence.

For many years we have watched the plea for help for those who are without food, shelter, and medical supplies on our television screens. In John's time in history, the poor could only buy the essentials in small measure. However for the wealthy, a continuing abundance of wine and oil must be preserved. Not much has changed in two thousand years.

It is good to note, crops of grain are much more likely to fail during a time of famine, where as the olive tree that produces the oil and the grape vines that bear the fruit for the wine, are more hardy and less likely to die. Yet the reference is still the same, look after those two aspects that only the wealthy can afford.

But what if the opening of the seal to the black horse has a different message? What if the black horse represents an inner famine, the famine of heart and soul? The oppression and control brought on by some religions can, and have, created the holding back of individual spiritual journeys, producing a time of fear and repression, a famine of journeying as spiritual beings. Particularly within Christianity, with the rise of both the catholic and protestant churches, nourishment for the soul and heart were metered out according to how their priests and leaders decided it ought to be.

I was brought up, as many were, with the mindset that unless I was a Christian and followed the path of religion set down by my parents, I was condemned to go to hell. How very arrogant to think that Christianity was the only doorway to heaven!

How very arrogant of any religion to believe they are the only ones whom God smiles upon, the chosen ones. In the vastness of the cosmos with its billions upon billions of planets, we are a very tiny link in the chain of planets and galaxies. Why would an amazingly powerful energy called God/ Great Spirit limit entry into heaven to such a minute number of people? I do not believe, there is a physical place called 'hell' to which we are sent if we disobey the rules of any religion. Hell is what we create in our lives when we stray from our path of the inner journey with our own spirit, and our link to the greater spirit.

To me, the black horse is a representation of the inner journey. Our outer journey within the world reflects what is happening within us. Our inner journey creates what happens within our outer journey. So let us not limit the nourishment of our soul and heart by only giving it small portions of what they need.

Let us not allow others to dictate to us how much of the grain we need to grow and expand into our greater selves; the abundant crop of divine love and creativity.

Verses 7 and 8:

7 "And when he had opened the fourth seal, I heard the voice of the fourth beast say, Come and see."
8 "I looked, and behold a pale horse; and his name that sat on him was Death, and Hell followed with him. And power was given unto them over the fourth part of the earth, to kill with sword, and with hunger, and with death, and with the beasts of the earth."

Some interpretations of these two verses attribute the vision of the pale horse, death, to the demise of the Roman empire. Within the following three hundred years the Roman empire fell by sword, from invaders and traitors within the empire itself. So, if this is what the pale horse was referring to, what relevance does it have to our modern-day beliefs and outcomes? Why did my dad, and others within the Christian religion, still relate at a personal level to what is written in The Revelation? As I have said before, I doubt if John and Yeshua were looking two thousand years hence with their prophecies.

And what of the fourth part of the earth? According to Edward Bishop Elliot (1793-1875; graduate of Trinity College, Cambridge; English clergyman and premillennial writer), who spent his life studying Biblical prophecies, the pale horse was a prophecy of a plague to come. The Plague of Cyprian raged from 250 AD to 265 AD. For a portion of that time five thousand people died every day in Rome. Many towns were wiped out. Rome's military hold on the people fell. Elliot saw the 'fourth part' as an indication of what was to come with the fall of the Roman Empire. Again, what relevance does this have to our modern-day spirituality?

As I sat with these verses, a thought process began to develop, as though I was being guided to see the writing in a different way.

The number four has been a deeply spiritual number for centuries through many cultures.

- The four elements – earth, water, fire, and air
- The four directions - north, south, east, and west
- The four beasts are seen in the corners of the Tarot card, The Wheel of Fortune, with wings
- We are made up of four parts – physical, mental, emotional, and soul.

The fourth horse, pale as if in death, speaks to me of the inner journey, our walk with the mental, emotional, and spiritual. And these three have their affect on the physical us.

It is only our physical self that dies. Our soul-self makes the transition out of the physical body back into the realm of spirit where we, once again, connect with our soul family. When we allow our deeper self to die we:

- Cut [sword] out of our lives those things that nurture and care for us, such as meditation, loving self, caring for our minds and hearts.
- Allow the plague of negative thoughts and feelings to crush us.
- We come into a place of deep hunger, seeking to be heard and understood; longing to be loved.

And what follows that inner death is our own self-made hell. We exist in our shadow-self instead of taking the adventure into our beautiful soul-self and discovering who we truly are.

Happiness is an inner journey. Nothing in our outer world can make us happy.

THE FIFTH AND SIXTH SEALS

The time has come for a massive change in the way we use the resources our beautiful planet gives to us; for us to honour her spirit; and to stop the violence toward her and toward our fellow human beings.

Chapter 6: 9 to 11

9 *"And when he had opened the fifth seal, I saw under the altar the souls of them that were slain for the word of God, and for the testimony for which they held;"*

10 *"And they cried with a loud voice, saying, How long Oh Lord, holy and true, doest though not judge and avenge our blood on them that dwell on the earth?"*

11 *"And white robes were given unto every one of them; and it was said unto them, that they should rest yet for a little season, until their fellowservants also and their brethren, that should be killed as they were, should be fulfilled."*

This fifth seal, when opened, spoke of the martyrs to come, those who would die for the cause of creating the Christian church in the bigger world – *"the souls of them that were slain for the word of God."* How sad. As a human race we have this inbuilt need to be right. Most religions throughout history have had their martyrs, those people who claimed to know what was true and real, and were killed in various ways for their proclamation. Why do we need to try and convert others to our truth? And why do we need to kill others for stating their truth? Where is understanding and unconditional love in that?

Some believed, and still do to this day, that in killing others of a different faith and culture, they were earning themselves a greater place in heaven. Really? What incredible power brainwashing has! I find it completely abhorrent that some religious group can manipulate a person's mind to the degree that they believe it is not only okay, but encouraged, to take the lives of others for Great Spirit's sake. Killing others for any reason is abhorrent, but to do it under the banner of religion and spirituality takes it to another level of maniacal homicide.

In the 10th verse we see the desire for retaliation. Hey Lord, when are you going to judge and punish them for making us martyrs? How many times throughout history have those who were treated badly turned around and became aggressors? We never learn. Gandhi and Nelson Mandela, they both saw the trap in revenge. They both said, don't do to them what they did to us. Rise above it and show the world the path of peace and reconciliation.

The 11th verse addresses the idea of 'karma'. What you give out comes back to you, every time. The martyrs were given white robes to wear as a sign of their need to be cleansed of their pain, and to step into the purity of their spiritual journey as souls seeking out their own truth. They were then told not to be concerned about what was going to happen to their aggressors; to rest from all that negativity. Then comes an interesting statement:

"... until their fellowservants also and their brethren, that should be killed as they were, should be fulfilled."

In other words, those who turned against you and killed you, your fellowservants and your brethren, because of the cosmic laws of karma, they in turn will also be killed. What you give out comes back to you – every time.

The laws of karma are not about revenge, they are about balance. These verses put me in mind of my dad's journey with me.

I once did Brandon Bays' exercise, "The Journey". It takes you back from your current time, all the way back to being in the womb, and still further back into spirit before conception. It allows you to access information held within your subconscious mind of events and conversations you may have forgotten at a conscious level; to know what was set in place as your life purpose before you were conceived; to understand conversations heard within the womb that may bring clarity and understanding; and to see the path of pain up to the current time that requires healing.

What I understood so very clearly when I came out of The Journey, was that my dad and I had been battling it out for centuries in the round-about of karma. One lifetime he would be the aggressor, then in the next I would be the aggressor. It had to stop. It had to stop in this lifetime. And because I was the one with the knowledge, it was up to me to create the healing between us. It was my place to heal the wounds I felt he had inflicted on me through his religious dogma. I was able to see what had created those many lifetimes of aggression was fear. I went to see my dad who was now eighty-six years of age. I spoke openly, but gently of the struggle we had been through. I told him of the pain I had felt, but I also told him I understood why. He told me of his fears for me, and how that had caused him pain. Without talking about past lives or karma, I simply said, "It has to stop dad, for both of us. We have to stop pushing against each other. Let love be our guide. I do love you, but for too long I have been trying to get your acceptance. For too long you have been trying to change me into who you want me to be out of fear for my welfare. I am not the person you want me to be, and neither are you the person I have judged you to be. Let us bring this to an end and allow love to be present for the rest of our lives." He nodded, smiled, and said, "Okay." And then asked if I would like a cup of tea. With those few words, centuries of karmic counterbalancing came to an end.

Such was the message in this vision of the martyrs... don't seek revenge. The aggressors will continue on their karmic journey. All you need to do is rest, rejuvenate, come into peace, and let go of the need for revenge, for it serves no purpose, and only keeps you going around in circles of aggressive and hurtful behavior.

Verses: 12 to 17

When the sixth seal was opened, what John and Yeshua saw was the coming of earthquakes, with mountains and islands moving out of place, an eclipse of the sun, meteorites falling to our planet, with people of all levels of society seeking shelter from the catastrophes taking place around them. And so it has been for two millennia. This age we now find ourselves in continues the devastation, and all of our own making.

Earth, herself, has been sending us the warning for at least a century. If we don't stop our abuse of her, creating an imbalance in her wilderness, destroying the very habitat that supports us, we will know her wrath. We have not listened enough. Nostradamus tried to warn us. We did not listen. So here we are with famine, floods, fires, earthquakes, cyclones, our polar ices melting, droughts, species of animals dying out, and never a day without war and aggression somewhere on our planet. The imbalance is huge. The time has come for a massive change in the way we use the resources our beautiful planet gives to us; for us to honour her spirit; and to stop the violence toward her and toward our fellow human beings.

Still within the sixth seal, in chapter seven, John is given a glimpse into life beyond death. As tragedies upon our restless planet come and go, and people die, they return back to their soul families in spirit. Here he sees that heaven is not limited to a particular race of people; that no one race are the chosen ones; that all of mankind has entry into the realm of spirit we call heaven. Verse nine of chapter seven states:

"After this I beheld, and lo, a great multitude, which no man could number, of all nations, and kindreds, and people, and tongues [languages], stood before the throne, and before the Lamb [Yeshua], clothed with white robes; and palms in their hands."

Why did they carry palm leaves in their hands in this vision? The branches of the palm trees seem to have a lot of significance at that time. On Yeshua's entry into Jerusalem, one week before he was crucified, his followers saw in their prince the potential for him to overthrow the Romans. Remembering, it was not the Romans who sent Yeshua to his death, but the political leaders from his own Jewish community. The Jewish leaders also saw his potential to become a political leader and have sway over the people, and they were having none of it.

The palm tree had many uses:

- The fruit from the date palm
- The making of brooms

- Shade
- Fans for the hot weather
- Dried or dead they were fuel for fires

And here, in this story, the palm branches were used as a carpet to cover the dust of the road, and to signify how they saw Yeshua as a leader, not only spiritually but politically. So to come before Yeshua, back in spirit, with the leaves of palms in hand, they were letting him know he was still their leader.

Verse 13 and 14:

13 *"And one of the elders answered, saying unto me [John], What are these which are arrayed in white robes? And whence came they?"*

14 *"And I said unto him, Sir, thou knowest. And he said unto me, These are they which came out of great tribulation, and have washed their robes, and made them white in the blood of the Lamb."*

Remembering, the Elders were the highly evolved beings who sat within Yeshua's council of twenty-four. So it seems he was testing John's understanding of what was happening because the Elders surely knew what it was all about.

These were the martyrs of the new religion, Christianity, and followers of Yeshua who had died and returned back to spirit where their leader now resided. White being the symbol of healing and purity; the symbolism of the people washing their garments until they became white in the blood of Yeshua, [hardly a way to create white garments], is a representation of love cleansing away all the trauma, pain, and ugliness of the past.

Yeshua did not fight against the authorities, neither Roman nor Jewish. If he had wanted to, his following was such he probably could have raised his own army and fought against both of them. But that was not his journey on this planet. His soul's purpose was to bring love and healing to the planet; to awaken people to their deeper selves; to prove to us that we have incredible power within us to overcome adversity, to create miracles and heal ourselves and others.

John reports that our work is not completed when we die and move back into the spiritual realms. Life goes on, and we continue to be of service to others and in service to that magnificent and magical powerful energy I call Great Spirit.

Verses 16 and 17:

16 *"They shall not hunger no more, neither thirst anymore; neither shall the sun light on them, nor any heat."*

17 *"For the Lamb which is in the midst of the throne shall feed them, and shall lead them into living fountains of waters; and God shall wipe away all tears from their eyes."*

The reference to the sun and heat is to say that they have left the physical world behind. Night and day no longer have an influence upon them. The idea of being hot, cold, hungry, or thirsty will no longer exist.

Again we have here the words, *"in the midst of the throne"*, meaning in the midst of the seat of power… within the power base of spirit. And here, all sadness, pain, and grief, will no longer exist.

"shall wipe away all tears from their eyes."

And so it is!

13

THE SEVENTH SEAL

True and lasting power comes from wisdom, compassion, understanding, and love.

We come to the last of the seals to be opened. The Biblical writings of the seventh seal are long, beginning with chapter eight of The Revelation and ending in chapter twenty-two [inclusive], the end of the book of The Revelation. Obviously, if I were to comment on every verse within those fifteen chapters the reader would become somewhat bored, and the volume of work would be enormous. So I provide an overview of the events that take place in the prophecy and visions John saw, and how they can relate to each of us today.

A lot of what happens within these chapters is of a historical nature. Historians see the book of The Revelation as the prophecies of the downfall of the Roman empire. So what significance does that have for us today? At a political level, we have seen many empires fall since that of the Roman empire, and they will go on falling. As I write, the power base of the United States of America is eroding quickly. That particular 'Rome' will also fall, and possibly sooner rather than later. The Hitler empire of Germany rose and fell, and so it has been throughout history.

No empire or dynasty lasts forever. Why? When the ego decides to rule, rather than the wisdom of mind alongside the compassion of the heart, greed and the hunger for power implode upon themselves. And we are beginning to see such an implosion in America? On both sides of their political parties, one could guarantee there are rumblings going on in corridors and in offices of the White House; the backstabbing of party members who believe they can do a better job than their respective leaders. The imploding of that great nation has begun. Eventually, all empires come to an end. One of our Australian past leaders has been heard to say on national television, politics is personal. How right he is. Every leader must face those rumblings against them; the power-driven egos of the underdogs that want to bring such leaders tumbling down.

The same message applies at an individual, personal level. When we allow our egos to become our 'throne', our seat of power, we begin the process of imploding upon ourselves. True and lasting power comes from wisdom, compassion, understanding and love. True power lies within the eternal power of our spirit, encased in our soul. We are God/Goddess. We are part of the combined energy of that powerful force I call Great Spirit; that which others call God. When we separate ourselves out from that power base, and go it alone with our ego driven mind, we might know a temporary time of feeling triumphant in our outer world, but such a feeling of power has an emptiness to it that creates a hunger for more and more power, forever seeking something to fill the emptiness we feel inside.

From each of the remaining fifteen chapters I will seek to find the relevant message for our modern-day spiritual encounter with self, within our world, and with spirit. Come on the journey with me, and take what feels right for you from what I am guided to scribe.

FOUR OF SEVEN ANGELS

The power of love is, by far, the greatest power of all.

Chapter 8: 1-2

1 *"And when he had opened the seventh seal, there was silence in heaven about the space of half an hour."*

2 *"And I saw the seven angels which stood before God; and to them were given seven trumpets."*

As one can see, the number seven plays a major part in this book of Revelation.

- The seven new churches in Asia Minor [Turkey].
- The seven angels sent, one to each church.
- The seven candlesticks, one to each church. The Jewish candelabra that sits upon their altars has seven candles, the taller one in the center with three on either side.
- The seven seals.
- And now we have a further seven angels with seven trumpets, one per angel.

These seven angels were given the directive to bring about a major house cleaning of earth and of the Roman empire.

Seven has long been a significant number in spiritual, healing, psychic, and numerology terms.

- Seven was associated with the Greek goddess Athena and the Roman goddess Minerva.
- Seven represents the aspects of insightfulness, intuition, truthfulness, introspection, intellect, and wisdom. It is often associated with the crown and third eye chakras.
- In Biblical numerology, it represents completion or perfection.
- In modern numerology, based on ancient honoring's of the number 7, it is seen as an angelic number with messages coming from the Universe. It is the number often associated with shamanism, and mediumship workers .
- In Tarot, the seventh card of the Major Arcana is the chariot, moving forward, with power, and being triumphant.
- In Theta Energy healing, the healer, [in a state of theta], moves through the seven realms, beginning with Earth, into the eternal realm of source. To name a few…

The first angel sounded his trumpet and brought to earth, hail, fire, and the burning of a third of the trees and grasses. Sound familiar? Here in Australia we have been living with such phenomena for many years. Floods and fire are our catch cry every spring, summer and autumn. Back two thousand years ago, the vision John had was only that of where the Romans ruled, a relatively small area when you consider the rest of the world. The 'one third' that keeps repeating throughout this eighth chapter is in reference to the area the Romans occupied, one third of the lands and towns of the countries they had invaded.

As within, so without. As without, so within. Our outer world is a reflection of our inner journey with self, and our inner world is always reflected in how we are coping with life. We also have to know the cleansing effects as we grow into our greater selves, our soul-self. Fire and ice, [hail], are the opposites of each other. All of life has a duality; night and day, the shadow self, [ego], and the light self, [spirit]; storm and calm; vibrancy and dullness; fear and peace; hatred and love; joy and sorrow. Fire has the ability to burn off that which no longer serves us, but it also holds the passion for all that we do. Hail cleanses in a different way; its harsh pelting can be devastating to plant life, but once melted it can replenish a thirsty earth. Often, that which seems to be negative, can have a blessing we cannot see.

I was born in the star sign of Gemini – the twins. Gemini people are here to learn about duality; to overcome the negative and step into the positive; to become the alchemist, turning the basis of what we have into beauty, strength, and durability. We have a choice, as all people do, to sit sadly in the negative, or use the experience to learn, grow, and be lifted up into our greater self.

John saw a vision with this first angel of a massive cleansing, rather like we are currently seeing. Mother Earth has a way of saying enough is enough. We have just been through a plague worldwide called Covid, followed by fire, floods, and cyclones.

When the second angel blew his trumpet, volcanoes erupted and the molten lava ran into the sea. A third of the sea creatures died and a third of the ships were destroyed. The fish of the sea were an important part of the food chain for the people. Yeshua was also a fisherman, and it was with bread and fish that he fed the hungry crowds that gathered around him. To take out a third of the ships, presumably those of the Romans, would have been a crippling blow to their force.

Volcanoes are often associated with anger. Anger sometimes has its place, but when that anger has been smoldering over a long period of time, it will eventually erupt into something destructive to all concerned. That which nourishes us – love – is lost to the power of anger.

When the third angel's trumpet sounded, a meteorite fell into the waters: *"there fell a great star from heaven, burning as if it were a lamp."* The waters became bitter with the taste of minerals and burnt matter, not to mention the incredible mess it would have made! Large numbers of people died because of the polluting of the water.

Many cultures see meteorite stones to be sacred, representing emotional support, balance, physical healing and spiritual growth. Why? Because of their association with the cosmos, bringing to our planet energy and minerals not available here. The cosmic energy connecting with our energy. The connection to all that is.

When the sound of the fourth angel's trumpet rang out within John's vision, a third of the sun and a third of the moon eclipsed. That part of the earth, which lay under the eclipsed third of the sun and moon, fell into darkness. An indication that the Roman rule would come to an end, but what would bring it to an end would be the darkness within the hearts of those who hungered for power.

Power gained through the darkness of thought and deed is unsustainable. The power of love is, by far, the greatest power of all. The rulers throughout history who were greatly loved, were those who ruled from a place of compassion and the desire to understand and help their people. They ruled from a place of light. Those who rule from a place of fear, anger, and darkness eventually implode upon themselves, as Hitler did, and as will our modern-day rulers who are creating angst around our planet.

And so it is at a personal level. You want to be loved? Then love others. If you are wondering why others do not love you, then be brave and take a look at what you are projecting out from your ego self. Make the shift to change what is happening within you to a positive energy, then watch love come flooding into your life. What you give out comes back to you, every time!

Such was the prophecy John was seeing. Those who ruled from a place of darkness would ultimately struggle in the darkness they created.

15

DISBELIEF

Let us live in peace.

Chapter nine of Revelation is one of horror and ugliness. Before we go any further into these accounts of what John saw, I have questions to ask. I feel you should ask the same questions. After all, Yeshua came to speak and show the truth of a loving soul. I am not one to take for granted what someone has written as the full truth. My questions are:

- Are these visions actually what John saw? They do not fit with a Yeshua who came to this planet to bring healing, love, and light. Do these images fit with a "just and loving God"? Yeshua could get angry and upset just like any other human being, but he was not a vengeful soul. Never did he cross the line into physical abuse or torment. Nor did he feel the need to defend his own truth. He came to share a different vision based on divine love.
- As I stated in the first chapter, the Bible has been translated several times through different languages. How much have these visions changed through

translation? And have they been deliberately changed through the ages to fit with the Christian churches control over people, using such visions to place the people into a state of fear and obedience? During the Dark Ages, corruption reigned within the Catholic Church; the popes ruling as kings, the licentious priesthood with its moral hypocrisy preaching the fear of losing one's life to hellfire and damnation if you didn't bow to their rule. This is only now starting to break down.

We also need to remember, as the historians believe, what John was supposedly seeing was the fall of the Roman empire. And, for the most part, the visions were symbolic, if somewhat disturbing.

As I read and reread chapter nine, I could see no relevance to our modern day, until I began to look at the wars that have taken place on Earth since 1900, and the many from before that time. I counted, from the list presented by The Australian War Memorial, between 1900 and 2017, there have been two hundred and sixty-seven wars. From 2017 to the end of 2023, there have been ten. Millions of people have died and been tortured during that time. The figures are staggering.

Astrology needs to reassess whether Mars truly is the planet of war. In this galaxy, it is planet Earth that is the warring planet. Beings from spirit and from other realms must shake their heads in dismay to see such evidence of ego-driven power, self-destruction, and the silent voice of the common people, who fail to stand up and say… no more war, no more war! Let us live in peace!

At this point in examining The Revelation, I believe it will be helpful to remember the difference translations can make, such as the example of the Lord's Prayer as shown in the first chapter of this book.

Chapter nine is a hellish chapter. I personally do not believe in a place called Hell, [which is the inference in this chapter], regardless of the teachings of my dad. He meant well, and always feared for my wayward soul, but my encounter with spirit as a medium has never seen such a place. Hell is what we have created here on this planet. Hell is the darkness within our minds and hearts. What we think and believe we create. I must say it a thousand times over in the space of a year, and the power of that wisdom never lessens. It is a truth that has been with us since the beginning of time. This truth not only works at a personal level, but it also works within the greater community. Sir Winston Churchill used this truth to great effect during the Second World War when he told the people of Britain… we will not fail… and they believed him.

However, I do embrace the idea of accountability. Each of us came to live on this planet to grow, gain greater wisdom, to find and step into the beautiful spirit energy that is held within our deeper soul-self, to understand and practice the art of unconditional love, and to serve our fellow people. When we climb out of the car we are driving around in called the body, and walk back through the gates into our spirit home, we will go through a life review. It is not about judgement, [as some religions would have it], but taking account of how well we did, or not, according to the contract we agreed to before entering this life. The next level of excellence we go to as part of our soul's ongoing education depends on this life review.

As I write, the wars between Russia and the Ukraine, and Israel and Palestine rage. Other skirmishes are also present in the middle east, and closer to home, China is flexing its muscles. Do we ever learn?

Chapter nine of revelation is still very much present with us. The vision John had in this chapter was for a five-month period of disaster on our planet. Little did he know that such disasters were going to continue for two thousand years and beyond.

16

THE VOICES

For those of us who have freedom of speech, it is so important to be standing in the place of divine light as we share our messages.

Chapter 10: 3-4

3 *"And cried with a loud voice, as when a lion roareth; and when he had cried, seven thunders uttered their voices."*

4 *"And when the seven thunders had uttered their voices, I was about to write; and I heard a voice from heaven saying unto me, Seal up those things which the seven thunders utters, and write them not."*

Thunder, especially for the Jewish and Greek people, was the voice of God. Here we have eight voices; the one that sounded like a lion roaring, announcing that there was more to come, and seven voices bigger and greater than the first. Each voice spoke a truth to John. Note, this was not a singular voice such as that of a singular being called God. These were seven separate voices - *seven thunders uttered their voices*. And here we have the number seven again. Keeping in mind that number seven is a significant number in numerology and at a spiritual level. It is the number for a spiritual quest. It also means perfection, balance, and completeness. Seven is all about pursuing one's spiritual journey, connecting with our deeper self, and finding unity with the realm of spirit.

It is interesting that John was not permitted to write what he heard, such was the sacredness of what those beings had to say to him. Perhaps at that time the people were not ready to hear what Great Spirit had to say.

Later, in chapter ten, John is instructed to digest what they had told him. Symbolically the tenth verse says: *"And I took the little book out of the angel's hand, and ate it up; and it was in my mouth sweet as honey; and as soon as I had eaten it, my belly was bitter."* Put another way: At first what John heard from the seven voices sounded sweet, but the more he digested what had been said, the more he felt uneasy, squeamish, and perhaps a little fearful of the knowledge he was given.

In verse eleven, one of the angelic beings spoke with him: *"And he said unto me, Thou must prophesy again before many peoples, and nations, and tongues, and kings."* So the messages John received from these beings, he was instructed to hold within himself until such a time as he went on a journey through other countries telling them of the visions he had seen.

Prophesying is no longer limited to a few. In our time, we have many prophets around the planet. But one must remember, at that time the world was known to be flat, and their 'world' was much smaller than it is today. Countries like Australia and the Americas had not yet been discovered.

The instructions John received serve as a big reminder to our present prophets to never forget that they are a representative of the divine power of spirit. I have been known to enter into the field of prophesies, but each time it happens, I am aware of what a massive responsibility I have to make sure that what comes out of my mouth is accurate and not the imaginings of my ego self.

I suspect John felt the impact of being told to go and share the prophesies he had seen – *"my belly was bitter"*. Initially, the idea of being spirit's representative was sweet, like honey in his mouth. Then came the understanding of the importance of being accurate. He also knew that at times he would be putting his life at risk by sharing the knowledge that came to him from divine energy.

Our evolution out of the dark times, when to voice a truth that goes against religious or political dogma brought our lives into danger, has been a slow one indeed. For some cultures that threat is still present. More than ever, for those of us who have freedom of speech, it is so important to be standing in the place of divine light as we bring our messages to a planet that continues to be ravaged by the ego-driven power of war.

THE SHADOW AND THE LIGHT

*When we choose to get to know our deeper divine self,
we begin to find the light of love.*

Chapter 11: 3-4

In chapter eleven of Revelation two witnesses, [prophets], were sent to the city of Jerusalem to warn the people against the folly of not walking a spiritual life. For their efforts they were slain. In the seventh verse it says:

"And when they shall have finished their testimony, the beast that ascendeth out of the bottomless pit shall make war against them, and shall overcome them, and kill them."

The beast here, I believe, is a representation of the darker side of our inner journey made manifest in our outer world. One only has to observe on our television screens the carnage of war to understand what that beast can look like. I use war as an easy example of the beast, but there are many more examples of the beast at work:

- Family violence

- Murders
- Pedophilia
- Bullying
- Theft

To name a few. Every night in our news we see the workings of the beast referred to in this chapter of The Revelation. It is the dark, shadowy aspect, rising up from the negative aspects of our egos – the bottomless pit of our deeper, darker side.

'And shall war against them and kill them'. How many times throughout history has this happened? India's well-known spiritual leader, Gandhi was shot for his efforts, as was Dr Martin Luther King. I can still hear in my mind Nina Simone's song The King Of Love Is Dead.

"Once upon this planet earth lived a man of humble birth, preaching love and freedom for his fellow man. He was dreaming of a day peace would come to earth to stay, and he spread the message all across the land. Turn the other cheek he'd plead; love they neighbour was his creed. Pain, humiliation, death, he did not dread. Will the murders never cease? Are they men or are they beasts? What do they ever hope to gain? Will my country stand or fall? Is it too late for us all? And did Martin Luther King just die in vain?"

There is much more to the lyrics of this special song, but I wanted to share some of it, as it wraps up what chapter eleven is conveying. *'Are they men or are they beasts?'*, says it all. And we should be very aware that this is not gender specific. Women can also be beasts and need to seek out a better way of being.

Further on in the chapter, John tells of the resurrection of the two prophets. In verses eleven and twelve it is written:

"And after three days and a half the Spirit of life from God entered

into them, and they stood upon their feet; and a great fear fell upon them that saw them."

"And they heard a great voice from heaven saying unto them, Come up hither. And they ascended up to heaven in a cloud; and their enemies beheld them."

Does this sound familiar? On the third day Yeshua rose from the dead and ascended into heaven. Why the third day? Because the Jewish folk believe that a person's soul remains within the body for three days after death before ascending back into the realm of spirit. A good reminder that this Biblical text was not written by someone brought up in a Christian faith, but a man who was born into a Jewish family. And the visions he was receiving were given to him from Yeshua - who was also Jewish.

I have had personal experience of the three-day belief. When my husband died in 2002, my next-door neighbour, who was a close friend, and who was also Jewish, left me alone until the three days were over. His explanation was this:

"I did not wish to intrude because we believe the soul remains in the body for three days. The soul does this to give those close to that person time to adjust to the knowledge that the deceased is moving on."

Over the few days that followed his death, my husband's presence was very strong. There were many weird and incredible things that happened to a number of people. He shocked my son by showing himself as if he were here in physical form, and spoke to him saying, "Everything will be okay Rob. Your mother will be okay!"

As a nurse, being present for people who are dying, you get to feel, [and occasionally see], the soul energy of that person. As a medium, one never doubts the ongoing life of a soul.

Mediums get used to seeing people who have passed through the flimsy veil of death.

Ugly as this chapter may seem, there is also a message of hope towards the end. Heaven awaits our presence. But why wait until we are dead to understand and experience Heaven? The hell we create on this planet is created from the workings of dark minds and hearts. So it stands to reason, with the opposing forces of hell and heaven, that when we work from a mind and heart that are full of light, we create heaven in our lives. When we choose to get to know our deeper divine self, we begin to find the light of love, the greatest power of all. Our inner heaven, like our ethereal heaven, is waiting for us to walk out of the shadows of negative thoughts and feelings, and into the light of our beautiful soul.

Let us honour the deaths and ascensions of Yeshua, Dr Martin Luther King, Gandhi and so many others, who brought that singular message of love to us, and ensure that their lives and deaths were not in vain!

MARY

Seek the light of inner heaven.

Chapter 12: 1-2

1 *"And there appeared a great wonder in heaven, a woman clothed with the sun, and the moon under her feet, and upon her head a crown of twelve stars;"*

2 *"And she being with child, travailing in birth, and pained to be delivered."*

It is commonly believed the woman was Mary. The crown of twelve stars represents the twelve tribes of Israel. It is worthy to note, one inherits the Jewish life through the mother and not the father. A person can study to become a member of the Jewish community, but those born to a Jewish mother are automatically admitted into Judaism.

The second verse speaks of Mary being with child, delivering that child with a lot of pain. It is a reference to the beginning of the new church of Christianity and the troubles it would encounter as it was birthed on Earth. Here there is the follow-on from the Jewish belief that a person comes into a religious culture through the mother. And Mary is still seen as the mother of the Christian church, especially in the Catholic division of that religion. Mother Mary has equal place with Yeshua in the hearts of those followers. And in verse five we read that she brought into the world a man child who would be the ruler of this new religion - Yeshua.

In verse three, we have the appearance of a red dragon with seven heads and ten horns. The dragon was later referred to as the Devil or Satan [verse nine], not the fallen angel as is commonly thought, but a dragon. And that dragon was the Roman empire. On the Roman battle flag was displayed a red dragon.

The late Latin meaning for the word Devil or Satan is - *accuser or slanderer*. This castes a very different light on my perception of the Devil in my younger years. I think most Christians would see the Devil as the ruler of Hell, the tormentor, the one to be feared. These days, I see the Devil as being the inner journey of negativity within my own mind and heart, the battle within, not a spirit being as such. And in this sense, my own devil within does rule over the darkness I may at times fall into. The older I have become, the less I like that dark place inside of me, the more I seek the light of my inner heaven.

Interestingly, the red dragon across many cultures has quite positive attributes:

- Strength, determination, and power.
- Courage and bravery.
- Good luck and fortune.
- Fertility and abundance.
- Wisdom and spiritual growth.

Not quite what was intended in these written accounts of John.

In verse nine we are told that the dragon, [the Roman Empire], with seven heads was cast out into the earth. Most research sites agree, the seven heads represent seven political heads, seen later in Revelation as seven mountains of power, or seven kings. In this case, the red dragon and its seven political powers would bring persecution to those who would follow the new religion of Christianity.

I am grateful to be living in a country where I have the freedom to follow my own spiritual path without having to hide it for fear of persecution. Horrendously, in so-called modern times, we still have political and religious powers that demand the people of those states follow a certain religion. If they don't, they will be persecuted. And so the red dragon of The Revelation lives on.

THE BEASTS OF SEA AND EARTH

Be in a place of love and empathy for self and others.

In the thirteenth chapter, verses one to ten, John saw himself standing on the shore of a sea. Rising up out of the sea was a beast with seven heads and ten horns. The Beast again being the Roman empire.

Yet again we have reference to the ten horns. It is believed, by Biblical researchers and scholars, that the ten horns represent ten kings who have not yet obtained their domain but still hold power and sway over the communities. Some scholars believe they are the kings of different areas or countries of Europe as it was then known. Wherever they arose from, they had powers of persuasion and influence.

The seven headed beast that rose up out of the sea was like a leopard, with the feet of a bear, and a mouth like a lion. And here we have the seven headed beast, the seven domains with each of these heads having a particular power, [not dissimilar to seven ministers in a cabinet of a ruling government that have their portfolios, with a powerful leader]. If we take the symbology John has given us, it could look something like this:

- The leopard represents stealth, strength, and the ability to move quickly.
- The feet of a bear represent sure footedness, the power to hold something down, having a strong foothold on their territory.
- The mouth of a lion is the ability to roar and bring fear into peoples' hearts.

And the people worshipped the beast. In other words, the Roman empire, whilst feared, was held in high regard. No one was game to fight against such a ruling hand. The beast had seven kings on his team who held the attributes mentioned above. In addition to this, there were ten other kings-to-be, [princes?], who were working with the Roman empire.

Verse eight says – *And all that dwell upon the earth shall worship him, whose names are not written in the book of life of the Lamb slain from the foundation of the world.* Remembering that Yeshua was seen as the slain Lamb for the new religion of Christianity; back two thousand years ago, a lamb was slain in the Jewish temple as an offering to God to deliver the people from their darkness. Hence the reference to the blood of the slain Lamb, [Yeshua], delivering the people out of their darkness by establishing a new religion. To be not written in the Lamb's book of life, means they were not followers of the Christian faith.

In John's vision, the beast that rose up out of the sea, one could presume held power over the seas with ships, and the land edged by the sea.

Verses eleven through to eighteen tell of another beast coming up out of the earth. Verse eleven says – *"And I beheld another beast coming up out of the earth; and he had two horns like a lamb, and he spake like a dragon."* To speak like a dragon means he spoke like a Roman ruler. This particular beast, or leader, commanded the people to worship the first king – the ruler of Rome. This was a lesser king because he only had two horns, or two members of his cabinet. This particular leader could exercise all the powers of the king of the sea. But he chose to lead through deception, and by riding on the back of the first king - the ruler of Rome. One could surmise that he was a sycophant to the rule of the Roman empire. Those who chose not to worship Rome, this leader would kill. And so the persecution of the new Christians continued.

The last verse of Chapter thirteen has an interesting statement that is not resolved within the chapter. It says – *"Here is wisdom. Let him that have understanding count the number of the beast; for it is the number of a man; and his number is six hundred threescore and six.* A score is twenty – hence, six hundred threescore and six = 666. What is the significance of such a number is not stated. It is presumed the reader would know. A reference to Jewish numerology of that time. Then it meant:

- An adherence to a worldly or religious faith that is opposed to God.
- Refuses to follow the ten commandments.
- Someone who relies solely on the imperfect powers of their own self.
- One who walks in the darkness of the ego-driven power base.

Some people misinterpret it to mean the Devil's number. But that is not what this last verse says. It does not say this is the number of Satan or the Devil, [words used in the previous chapter], instead it says – *"for it is the number of a man."* This was the number of this particular ruler of the Roman empire. This is a man who rules from his ego-driven power rather than from a place of love. There is absolutely no mention here of it being the number of a spirit called Satan or Devil.

In Modern Numerology, 666 has many meanings. Here are a few:

- A triple number is influential; the repetitive number has added power to influence one's life. It is like driving the understanding of the number home to the one it is intended for, and also the energy of the number is stronger.
- Alter your focus, especially around your well-being with health and wholeness.
- Come into self-awareness and new growth.
- Be in a place of love and empathy for self and others.
- Synchronicity will begin to happen.
- Balance is needed.
- Redirect your attention to more fulfilling aspects of your life.

This single verse of eighteen is a good reminder; how life was perceived two millennia ago is not necessarily relevant to our more modern way of living and being, and our more enlightened understanding of the realm of spirit. Although, having said that, we still have leaders who demand of their followers that they worship within a certain faith, and/or adhere to a particular political governing body of people, and worship a certain leader.

20

BABYLON

Love is a far greater power than that of retaliation and resentment.

As a woman writing about this book of The Revelation, one could be greatly insulted reading the first five verses of chapter fourteen. Thankfully, we have come some way since men decided they were the superior race, and a woman was a second-class citizen. Yet we still have a long way to go within certain religions and cultures. In truth, all things considered, we have not come all that far in two thousand years.

For us women, the trap is to not do what was done unto us. The message of a great man now applies to women around the world as we continue to work towards a society of true equality and cooperation. Nelson Mandela said, "In the face of adversity, let us rise together, not against each other, but with compassion and understanding."

I am not one to believe in putting the opposite sex down. Women have been treated badly in the past, but that does not give women the right to become aggressive in return. Nothing is served by an eye for an eye; that only makes two blind people. We have seen how that works in political fields; those who were abused become the abuser and thousands of innocent lives are lost in the process. It is now our choice, as women, to bring enlightenment, understanding, and strength into this world; to aim for equality and make it a better world for all. Love is a far greater power than that of retaliation and resentment.

So, what is the statement that made me cringe as I read these five verses? John, in the vision presented to him, sees one hundred and forty-four thousand men gathered on the mount of Zion with Yeshua. These men were all virgins who, to quote from verse four:

These are they which were not defiled with women, for they are virgins.

That seems to me to be a bit of a backhanded slap to Mother Mary and Mary Magdelene, not to mention all the other women who had administered to Yeshua and his disciples. Again I question the validity of the interpretation from the original text. The Biblical meaning of the word defiled is unclean, impure and not worthy of God. These two Jewish men, Yeshua and John, who know that Judaism cannot exist without the women through which the line of Jewish culture descends. As such, surely such a statement could not leave their lips?

The rest of the chapter speaks of the fall of Baylon and the coming of Yeshua sitting upon a cloud. Cloud is a symbol for spirituality – of the air, misty, mysterious, the veil between worlds. Remembering that these were prophetic visions John was receiving, not a literal physical encounter of Yeshua sitting on a cloud. It is an indication that Yeshua would return to us through the realm of spirit.

My Protestant preaching dad would often speak of the second coming, the return of Jesus. Inside of me I would be screaming, "Oh for heaven's sake, can't you see? He returned within a very short time of his death." For me, his second coming does not relate to a physical life. Considering his prior experience, if he tried to do it again he would be considered blasphemous, a disturbed being, and would probably be locked away with a body full of drugs – if he wasn't shot first, like Gandhi. What worth is there in him returning as a human being, claiming to be the son of God? Like he was then, he would be ridiculed and would gain nothing. From my experience, seeing Yeshua and working with him as a master of light and healing, [not as a religious being], he has been with us since he left his body whilst hanging on the wretched cross. He is already back and has been for a very long time. If you are waiting for him to return as a physical being... good luck with that. You had better settle in for a long wait.

The fall of Babylon, as John prophesied, did take place. In the year 539AD, the Persians, [now known as the Iranians], took hold of Babylon, and a once admired, prosperous city, which at that time was the largest and wealthiest city in the known world, began to decline. The old city still exists today as a historical wonder and a destination for tourists.

21

THE SEVEN PLAGUES

Within us all is the greatest of powers – the power of divine love and creation.

Like a lot of chapters in this book of horrors, I read it and said to myself, "Joy, what on earth are we going to do with these next two chapters? How can this possibly be relevant to our modern understanding of God?" And then I heard the whisper of Yeshua's voice saying, "Remember it is a metaphor." My mind then went to all the wonderful authors we have had over the last century, and to my own understanding of the word 'God'. Perhaps the best understanding of the word 'God' comes within the writings of Neale Donald Walshe's books, Conversations With God and Godtalk. It is essential to understand, I believe, how that concept of a Great Spirit works for us before delving into the fifteenth and sixteenth chapters. To do so will bring a whole different story to the surface. Let me try and bring new life to what these ghastly chapters mean.

Here is my understanding of God, which I feel is closely aligned to Neale's understanding, and that of many other world-renowned writers. What others call God, I call Great Spirit. Neither God/ Great Spirit are a single being. They are the collective energy, the interwoven energy of all beings everywhere, who are standing within the light of the divine. God/ Great Spirit is the soul energy of us, all of us. The soul is of spirit, the ego is of humanity. The soul journeys through centuries and many lifetimes, here and on other planets, to gain wisdom, growth, and to learn to expand into its greatness. All souls everywhere are learning one basic lesson, how to love unconditionally both self and others, and to know the greater power of love over adversity. In short, our soul is pure; it is our ego driven mind that is not pure. We live with the dichotomy of dark and light, positive and negative, pain and joy – the opposites of soul and ego, that we may learn and grow into the fullness of our God energy, our spirit encased within our soul. When our spirit, which is pure energy, connects with other spirits, we then have the making of a Great Spirit/ God.

It is interesting to note whilst reading this chapter, that although John has since become a Christian, all of the visions and talk are seen through Jewish eyes – the temple and the tabernacle, not the church or the altar. Having not long returned to spirit, Yeshua was still in the mindset of his human life as a Jewish man as he brought these visions to John.

We return to number seven again. In this chapter we encounter a further seven angels. Remember, in the beginning of the Christian faith there were seven churches in Asia Minor, and to each church was assigned an angel. And now we have a further seven angels. In verse five and six it says:

"And after that, [the appearance of the seven angels], *I looked, and behold, the temple of the tabernacle of the testimony in heaven was opened;"*

"And the seven angels came out of the temple, having the seven plagues; clothed in pure and white linen, and having their breasts girded with gold girdles."

In chapter three of this book I wrote:

The number seven is a significant number in numerology and at a spiritual level. It is the number for a spiritual quest. It also means perfection, balance, and completeness. It is all about pursuing one's spiritual journey, connecting with our deeper self, and finding unity with the realm of spirit.

To each of these angels was given a golden vial within which was a plague. How interesting that the vials should be golden. Why gold rather than any other colour? It seems like such a contrast to the contents of the vials. Gold is seen as the metal and colour of abundance and divine status. If we relate this metaphor to us. As souls we a hold within us the energy of the divine, the Christ energy that relates to both our human self and our soul self. Whilst our souls are pure as of gold, within us, through our humanity, we hold the opposite to the divine. We are both light and dark.

Without the darkness, which is our teacher and challenger, we would not fully appreciate the divine light within us. The trick here is to not be swallowed up by the dark energy. For some peculiar reason, as human beings we have a propensity to wallow in the negative, yet we admire those great people who always preferred to walk in the beauty of the light. You hear people say, that is such a positive person; I don't know how they do it. They 'do it' because they have made a conscious choice to walk in their divine light rather than drown in pain, depression, and sorrow.

Moving into chapter sixteen of The Revelation, each of these angels in turn poured out of their golden vials the plagues upon the earth. So, what were these plagues and, as a metaphor, do they have any relevance to us?

- The first was a plague that brought with it annoying and painful sores. Humanity has continuously had such plagues throughout history – chicken pox, smallpox, measles, and more recently Covid.
  Message: cleanliness and caring for our environment, and caring for our bodies with healthy nourishment and activities.
- The second plague was poured on the sea, and *it became blood as a dead man*. War will do that. An infestation of dead people in the water as a result of sea warfare would attract sharks. The difference between then and now is that the attacking side does not see the devastation of their actions. We have become more sophisticated with our killing weapons, which has enabled a level of detachment from the lives we have taken. What does that say about us and our journey with fellow humans? We see it every day on our screens, the damage created by weapons fired from a great distance. Are our leaders becoming more detached from the people they serve? Do they not care for the damage that is created?
- The third angel did the same thing only with the rivers, and they also became *as with blood*.
- The fourth vial was of fire. [As I write - there are fires raging not far from where I live, and several towns are under threat. Evacuations are taking place.] Let us examine what that can mean for us at a personal level. Fire has opposing sides. In more modern-day spiritual language, fire means:

- Destruction leading to transformation;
- Cleansing leading to illumination;
- Purification into knowledge and truth;
- Passion, power, strength and rebirth; and
- Becoming an alchemist – the ability to transform from one state to another.

In The Revelation the author sees it as being the wrath of God. Well then, if God/ Great Spirit is all of us, we are surely on the path of destruction leading to transformation.

- The fifth vial was the plague of pain. Do you know anyone who does not carry pain of some kind? Pain is indeed a plague on this planet. Physical pain has its source in the mental and/or emotional bodies. Slowly, slowly scientists and the medical professions are seeing the correlation between what we think and feel, and how that effects our physical bodies. There are many wonderful books out now that can help you to align your thinking and feeling with what is happening at a physical level. The one I find the most helpful is The Key to Self-Liberation by Christiane Beerlandt – subtitled 1000 Diseases and their Psychological Origins. It is a book worth investing in to gain a deeper understanding of what we are going through at a physical level.
- The sixth vial was that of drought – the drying up of the river Euphrates. Within these verses, John refers to false prophets and those who do not speak the truth. I ask the question, what is truth? People experience different levels of understanding of philosophy, but there is a single truth that is the reality for us all, a truth that unites us if we could fully comprehend its power and significance. **That truth is this: within us all is the greatest of powers –**

the power of divine love and creation. We know the drying up of the river of life within us when we step away from the nourishing and nurturing waters of our soul in preference for the delusions of thought that takes us away from our soul's purpose – to be a happy, enlightened and loving being in service to our fellow mankind.

- The seventh vial was that of hail and earthquakes of great magnitude. There is nothing new about hail and earthquakes. Earthquakes have been with us since our planet was first formed. To look deeper at a spiritual level, it is the wakeup call. It is time for us beings on planet Earth to wake up from our slumber and learn to embrace the wonderful souls we are; to embrace our collective soul energy of the Christ within us, our God-self. It is time to shake things up a bit, to shift our perspectives, our perceptions, and to embrace a different way of being present with self and each other. Hail has been interpreted in many cultures and traditions to mean cleansing, transformation, and spiritual growth. In some cultures, rain on your wedding day is an omen for fertility, a happy marriage, and the cleansing away of all negativities. Hail, as the more solid form of rain takes these meanings to a deeper level.

Often that which appears to be negative can be something that brings about change in a positive way and helps us to see our lives from a different perspective – if we make the choice to wake up and embrace our inner light, our God-self.

22

THE SCARLET WOMAN

The time has come for all to change!

In chapter seventeen, John is taken on an ethereal journey by one of the angels to see – *"the judgement of the great whore who sitteth upon many waters; With whom the kings of the earth have committed fornication."* She is described as being dressed in Purple [royalty] and scarlet [earthy], adorned with gold and precious stones. This is a woman of wealth. But we are not talking about an actual woman here, that woman was Babylon – ruled by the Romans. The word fornication has a different meaning here. Another way of saying this would be... the kings of the areas associated with the Roman empire had climbed into bed with Rome. In other words, they had been brought under the spell of Babylon and her Roman rulers, and were willing to play along with the heads of the empire lodged in that city. It would be their undoing.

Again we have a reference to the beast with seven heads and ten horns. The seven heads representing the kings of seven countries, and the ten horns are the kings who as yet do not have a country, but still hold some power. The beast that is named in this chapter is again a reference to the Roman empire. The ten minor kings we would probably call princes.

Verse five of this chapter is a doozy. It is a description of Babylon and how the Roman empire had brought to other lands religious beliefs and political administrations that went against the Jewish and then the Christian beliefs. It says, in capital letters to emphasize the point:

And upon her forehead a name was written, MYSTERY, BABYLON THE GREAT, THE MOTHER OF HARLOTS AND ABOMINATIONS OF THE EARTH.

In the last verse of the chapter, John writes*: "And the woman which thou sawest is that great city which reigneth over the kings of the earth… Babylon."*

But like all empires, they have their day of glory, and then they fall. The hunger for power; the greed for material and financial wealth; and the desire to own other people's property eventually brings them down. There is no empire in the millions of years this planet has existed that has not fallen. Usually, they implode upon themselves through internal power struggles. Or the greed and hunger for power comes from an outside source, creating the downfall of those who have ruled. Nothing has changed. The struggle for power continues.

Change will only come when more and more ordinary people wake up within themselves and bring to the world the light of the divine Christ energy. And it is happening. All over this planet there are beautiful beings bringing the message of the power of love and the joyfulness of light to those who are asleep.

In all nations we see the rising up of spiritual souls from all walks of life, in many different forms, showing the way to that single truth – that we are all one. Writers, psychic folk, teachers, healers, philosophers, workshops, music to help us meditate or sleep in peace, Red Cross workers, doctors without borders, presenters such as David Attenborough – you name it, they are there working toward creating a world of peace and harmony. And the force of love is gathering momentum.

A few years ago, whilst in meditation, I was taken out into the cosmos. From there I could look back at Earth. What I saw astounded me. It filled me with a sense of hope for our traumatized planet. Coming in from my right side I saw a large flow of energy. It was massive. It was white, but within that whiteness were the sparkles of all colours. It was an unstoppable force of love, healing, and cleansing. I felt its power and I heard, "The time has come for all to change!" When I found myself back in my normal human self, I felt a huge sense of peace and a deep stillness within me. Unbeknown to me, I had been crying with the awe and wonder of it all. Today, I am beginning to see the energy of that powerful source of love quietly moving amongst the people of our beautiful planet. It will keep on coming until we have all awoken to our true essence – our oneness with the greatest power of all. It is called love!

There is hope. Hang on to that hope. Get out of the negative thinking and help those who are working hard to create a world of peace and healing. Every tiny bit we do adds to the greater energy. Each of our souls are a fragment of Great Spirit.

23

ANCIENT WISDOM

What you put out comes back to you – every time.

An interesting thing about wisdom, it never goes backwards. It increases as us lesser human beings grow, awaken, become more insightful, reclaim our soul essence, and gather understanding, compassion, and knowledge. But wisdom itself is as ancient as all the universes.

One piece of that ancient wisdom which has never changed and is still as relevant today as it was millions of years ago; wisdom that many before me, myself, and many to come will keep on trying to get through to the collective consciousness is:

What you put out comes back to you – every time.

Are you tired of hearing it? Then begin to truly hear it; not as words in your head, hear it in your heart. Put out negative thinking and feeling and you will create a negative world for yourself. Put out hate and hate will return in greater measure. Put out love and it will come flooding back to you – every time. God/ Great Spirit is not the creator of your success or mess. You are. Pure and simple. God/ Great Spirit will support you with all of your decisions about your life. If you say I am unworthy to be loved, spirit will respond with okay - if that is how you feel. It's a bit sad that you feel that way, especially as we had all these people lined up to love you; but if that is your belief, then so be it. If you say [and believe] I am worthy of great love and I have a lot of love to give, spirit's response will be... YEAH! Here, have some more love. Why? Because you have created the space to allow love to become an integral part of your life.

Why do I say this is ancient wisdom? Because chapter eighteen of The Revelation is all about this piece of wisdom. It is about the fall of Babylon, the greatest of cities at that time. Why did she fall? *What she put out came back to her.*

In verse two an angelic being says to Paul in a vision of prophecy – *"Babylon the great is fallen, is fallen and is become the habitation of devils."* And then in verse eight, the same angel says [speaking of Babylon] – *"Reward her even as she has rewarded you, and double unto her double according to her works; in the cup which she hath filled fill to her double."*

As said in the previous chapter, most political and materialistic seats of power eventually implode upon themselves through the hunger for power and greed. And here we have the prophecy that what Babylon gave out – greed and hunger for power – came back to her in double strength. The rulers of Persia took over Babylon and she was never the same again. In verse eleven the angel says to John: *"And the merchants of the earth shall weep and mourn over her; for no man buyeth their merchandise anymore."*

Then follows a few verses describing what abundance Babylon once offered. In verses fifteen to seventeen, the angel tells John:

"The merchants of these things, which were made rich by her, shall stand afar off for the fear of her torment, weeping and wailing,"

"And saying, Alas, alas, that great city, that was clothed in fine linen ,and purple, and scarlet, and decked with gold, and precious stones, and pearls:"

"For in one hour so great riches is come to nought; and every shipmaster and all the companies in ships, and sailors, and as many as trade by sea, stood afar off."

In Babylon's hour of destruction, those who had gained from her power and greed, the merchants, fled the scene and took their merchant ships out to sea away from the horrendous fall of a city that once made them financially wealthy.

In verse twenty-three the angel, as if speaking to Babylon herself, said:

"And the light of a candle shall shine no more at all in thee; and the voice of the bridegroom and bride shall be heard no more at all in thee; for thy merchants were the great men of the earth; for by thy sorceries were all nations deceived."

Here, the message is simple. Deceive others and eventually you can expect them to walk away from you. The pain and darkness of loneliness will find you without even the light of a candle. Live in truth and with honesty and your light will continue to shine.

I have seen a classic example of the evidence of such a simple statement. I once had a woman who used to come to a meditation class I facilitate. Her whole attitude was one of what can I get out of this, rather than what can I contribute to this gathering of people. The others in the group became weary and frustrated with her continuous complaints that she was not understood and that she was lonely. Regardless of the multiple efforts the others made to engage with her, the invitations to have a chat over coffee, and the endless feedback they lovingly gave her about her worth as a beautiful woman, she continued to tell them she had no friends, and they didn't care about her or understand her.

The woman's self-deception that she had no friends, and the deception she fed to the others about her life, about how poor she was when she lived in a beautiful home, became a source of irritation. Eventually what she believed - she created. They all stopped trying to engage with her. The invitations for coffee and a chat ceased. When she spoke, the room fell silent. No one responded. She left the group feeling lost, lonely, and unwanted. Two weeks later she rang me to say how hurt she was that no one wanted to be friends with her. I asked of her, "How many times have you invited someone into your home, or even down the street to have a cup of coffee with you and a chat?" Her answer was, "When they ask me I will ask them." I replied, "But they did ask if you would like to join them for coffee and a chat. You didn't follow through with an acceptance. Perhaps, if you began by welcoming people into your life, rather than waiting for them to do it, you might begin to find people will open their hearts to you." She hung up.

Self-deception is a real block for many people. To deny the beauty within you – your light shining within your soul – creates a hunger for outer acknowledgement and acceptance, always trying to fill the emptiness with - *clothed in fine linen ,and purple, and scarlet, and decked with gold, and precious stones, and pearls.* Nothing in our outer world can take the place of learning to love and accept self.

In the words of the angel - *Babylon the great is fallen, is fallen and is become the habitation of devils.* Such devils is what we know inside of us when we choose, as this lady did, to create a life from our negative thoughts and feelings. Inside of us we create the devils of lack of self-worth, loneliness, and an isolation from love and friendships. We create an isolation from the God within. But we have the ability to change that.

24

THE BRIDE AND GROOM

When we stand in the light of our divine soul we will know victory and peace.

In chapter nineteen, we now begin to see a shift away from the imagery of horror to more pleasant visions for John that Yeshua was giving him. The first few verses see a celebration in his prophecies, with the fall of one of the Roman empire's strongholds - Babylon. Then in verse seven we have an interesting account of the Lamb [Yeshua] being prepared for a wedding.

"Let us be glad and rejoice, and give honour to him; for the marriage of the Lamb is come and his wife hath made herself ready."

Yeshua's bride was the new church of Christianity. He was showing John, with the breaking down of the Roman empire, that Christianity could now flourish and a new contract between the people and himself could begin.

I always find it interesting that the very empire, which created for the newly formed church of Christianity so much grief with the killing of its martyrs, should end up having the headquarters for the Catholic Church in Rome. It is also interesting to note, a lot of the pageantry and symbolic use of incense, candles, and regalia was borrowed from Jewish traditions.

For one sector of Christianity, Rome still holds the power. And from that seat of power, the Christians committed the very same atrocities against people of other beliefs. From the 1450s to the 1750s, witches were hunted down and killed in horrendous ways, both in Europe and America. The Catholic Church claimed that witchcraft was heresy and set about purging the community of their faith. For three hundred years it went on – roughly the same time that it took for Christianity to rise up out of its abuse by the Roman's and Jewish people. And behind both was the power of Rome.

In verses eight and nine we read:

"And to her was granted that she should be arrayed in fine linen, clean and white; for the fine linen is the righteousness of saints."

"And he saith unto me, Write, blessed are they which are called into the marriage supper of the Lamb. And he saith unto me, these are the true sayings of God."

Remembering that the true definition of church is a gathering of people – not a building. So if God is not a singular being, but an energy that resides in all of our souls and connects us to all that exists within the cosmos; then what Yeshua is saying in this statement is this:

His new bride - the people who have become his followers through Christianity – will find within them the love [Christ energy] that all the saints and martyrs found deep within their soul-self. These are the ones who died over the first three hundred years of the birth of Christianity at the hands of the Jews and Roman rulers, because of their belief in a new way forward. They will find the purity of that love and healing that can be likened to *"fine linen, clean and white."* And they will know the truth within them [*the true sayings of God*] of that deep and eternal love.

In verse ten John falls to his knees at Yeshua's feet. But Yeshua responded with – *"And he said unto me, See thou do it not; I am they fellowservant, and of thy brethren."* Yeshua was giving John the message that he was the servant of mankind and did not wish to be worshiped as another god. In addition, John was Yeshua's biological brother.

It is a lovely thing to do, to give reverence to those who have walked a path of service to mankind. But are we not all in service to mankind? So, do we revere our own soul as we do the soul of others? All of the great souls who have walked this planet would say the same thing as Yeshua; do not bow before me for I am in service to humanity as you are; you are just as important as I. Moses, when he led his people out of Egypt into their new home, as they entered that place he held back, choosing not to go with them. His job was done. And I strongly suspect he did not wish to be worshipped as a king would be. After all, he had just taken his people out of a kingdom that was destructive for them. He quietly left and went in a different direction.

I have often said to those who participate in my workshops, "Be careful of the power of your ego. The moment you step into thinking you are better than others, more important than others, more knowledgeable than those around you, the true power of your soul begins to diminish. The man who picks up my garbage is just as important as the greatest leader. Without him doing his job, the greatest leader would be living in squaller and probably die of some ghastly disease."

There is no better than; there is only a soul's life purpose. It is the ego that wants 'better than'. And, it is our lack of acknowledgement of our own soul's greatness that makes us place another on a pedestal. Yeshua knew that better than anyone. He also knew that when you place someone high up on a pedestal two things happen:

- The person on the pedestal is likely to get knocked off their stand when things don't go the way we want them to; and
- It is hard to communicate with people when you have to shout at them from way up high.

As a facilitator of workshops on psychic abilities, and of meditation classes, one of the things I am constantly saying to people is that your guides do not want to be separated from you by being placed on a pedestal or kept at arm's length. They want to get up close and personal with you. Keeping them in the place that John began to place Yeshua means it is so much harder for them to work with you, through you, and for you. They want to be your closest and dearest friend. And love, when it comes to your guides, is not a one-way street. They love you all the time. Learn to love them ALL the time. The closer you bring them to you, the more of a team you become, and the more you will achieve in all manner of achieving.

From verse eleven through to the end of chapter nineteen, we have visions of Yeshua taking his place within the power seat of heaven. He is seen as riding a white horse, [purity], and, likewise, those who follow his example also dressed in fine, white linen and riding white horses. In his mouth is a sword; the sword of truth and victory.

And what is Yeshua's victory? It is simple. Where light exists darkness cannot exist. Truth always prevails over deceit. Love always conquers hate. And when we stand in the light of our divine soul we too will know victory and peace. There is no greater power than the power of love.

And what is the truth? We are all one!

25

THE BOTTOMLESS PITT

Our growth and learning never ends.

And now we come to the infamous chapter twenty of Revelation. The creation of hell.

I personally find this chapter to be one of the most misunderstood and ill-used chapters of them all. My dad and I had many interesting discussions around the imagery of this chapter. They usually ended in him shaking his head and telling me I was a lost soul. When I was a teenager these images were frightening, but the further I moved into adulthood and began to think through what the images might mean, the further away I moved from my dad's interpretation of hellfire and damnation. The more I stepped into communication as a medium with beings in spirit, the more convinced I became that chapter twenty was a metaphor for our inner journey with self.

Hell is what we create when we allow the ego to rule through negative thoughts and feelings. In our modern age, depression and anxiety have become common conditions in our communities. And what we feel within us, we create in our outer world. Feeling victimized and punished is not about others; it is what we have created within our own energy. What we believe we create. We are magnificent creators. If we create within us the idea of being victimized, that is exactly what will happen to us. If we create within us love towards others and a wholeness within self, then love is what will flow back to us. For me, both hell and heaven are of our own making.

I no longer believe in a bottomless pit, a place called hell, where we are sent if we do not bow down to Christianity and to Yeshua. I am quite certain there may be plenty of planets, stars, suns, or moons within the multiverse that could look and feel like this supposed vision John received. And I have a question about imprisoning a being called the Devil or Satan in a bottomless pit. If the pit is bottomless, how can anyone be contained in it? Surely they would eventually find their way out if it was bottomless. And my reason for asking such a question? Is this what was truly said by John, or were other words used that have a very different meaning, as we have seen with the Lord's Prayer.

In the second verse is written:

"And he [an angel] *laid hold on the dragon, the old serpent, which is the Devil, and Satan, and bound him a thousand years."*

The dragon was the symbol used on the ensigns of the pagan Roman Empire. A little bit of information which is conveniently forgotten when religious folks are preaching from this chapter. What John was seeing was a metaphor for the number of years the dragon, the Roman Empire, would be held down without power over the nations. The dragon, otherwise known as Devil or Satan, was not a nasty spirit being, but the power of the Roman empire and its adherence to pagan gods. This brings a whole different understanding to this chapter when seen in this light.

How effective was this? Instead of Rome killing off the Christians because they did not adhere to their pagan gods, they decided to flip the coin. They became the Christians who then decided to kill off those who worshipped pagan gods. In both cases, Rome ruled from a place of fear. And the fear of hellfire and damnation is still being used against people today to control them and create obedience to Christianity, and also to Islam, whose religion also uses the threat of a burning hell.

From verse seven onward, John sees visions of a power coming from the four corners of the earth. The concept of earth then was a much smaller one than what we know today. Then it was believed the Earth was flat, and lands such as the Americas and Australia had not yet been found by these people. In verse eight is written:

"And shall go out to deceive the nations which are in the four corners of the earth, Gog and Magog, to gather them to battle."

Again we are looking at a prophecy of another war to come.

So, what of Gog and Magog? Both names are old Russian words. Magog means Prince of Rosh. Rosh is the old root word for what we now know as Russia. Put another way, Magog means a princely nation or place; a land of greatness. And Gog is the person who rules over the land of Magog. When we look at what is happening today with Russia flexing her warring muscles, one can see a correlation between John's vision and our current situation in the world.

In verse twelve of chapter twenty, we see written:

"And I saw the dead, small and great, stand before God; and the books were opened; and another book was opened; which is the book of life; and the dead were judged out of those things which were written in the books, according to their works."

The first thing that speaks to me within this verse is - *And I saw the dead, small and great, stand before God.* Death is a great equalizer. We may see ourselves as either small or great in our world, but when it comes to leaving our physical form, [the car our soul has been driving around in during our human life], and leaving behind our ego, there is no small and great, we are all one of the same star dusts from which we are created.

The second aspect of this verse, which I find validating for my belief is – *"and the books were opened; and another book was opened; which is the book of life."* Here we have reference to what is now known as the Akashic Records. These records are not a new concept. That concept goes a long way back into BC. There is reference to them in the Old Testament of the Bible; in Exodus 32:32 and several times in the psalms. What of these books?

The reference to the first 'books' is our individual records of our lives throughout many incarnations. They hold within them how our souls have journeyed; our achievements, what we learned, what we failed to learn, and what corrections are needed in our next incarnation. Our growth and learning never ends. We are all on the road to our ultimate goal of complete wholeness and state of the I am-ness. Even great masters like Yeshua are still learning. The Bible uses the word judgement. In our more modern understanding of the word 'judgement' is the word 'assessment'. So when we decide to leave the car we have been travelling around in, [our bodies], and return home to our spirit family we go through an assessment of how our journey on Earth went. It is not a judgement as such, as Christianity would have it, of whether you go to hell or heaven. It simply allows us to know how well, or not, we fulfilled our souls contract to grow and learn, and to be of service to our people. It sets a guideline for what we will need to achieve in our next incarnation.

The second book referred to – *"and another book was opened; which is the book of life"* – is the combined records of all people. Another way of describing this could be that our individual records of the first book then become chapters within the second book, the book of life. Now, none of these books are actually in physical form. That would be one massive library. They are all in the form of energy; an energy that is accessible to all people through meditation or some other form of going deeply to connect with those lives, such as hypnosis. Both Dr Brian Weiss and Dr Michael Newton have been experts in this field of recall through hypnosis. These books are a vibrational energy, believed to exist in the fifth dimension.

A word of warning. If you are seeking to find out what has happened to you in a previous life, remember:

- To make sure you have a fully qualified practitioner that you can trust.
- This is not a game but a serious look to the past to heal the present.
- What you see, be it a king or beggar, makes no difference to who you are now, except for you to understand what is happening for you at a deeper level, and to learn from that experience.

What John was seeing in this vision was the understanding that, regardless of what part we play on this planet, we all are brought to an equal level through death. We all have to account for the journey we have taken when we pass through that fine veil of death. And we are all here to learn, grow, and be of service as unique and beautiful souls.

THE NEW JERUSALEM

We are simply returning to a knowledge we once lost.

There is a theory; whatever you perceive the afterlife to be, that is what will be created for you. Is there truth in this? I have no idea. None of us can truly know until we get there. It is a theory. But for me, I am happy to go along with the theory and create in my mind an astonishingly beautiful and magical place, filled with love, colour, music, and creativity. Occasionally, I get a tiny glimpse into the afterlife, and the colours I see, and the music I hear leave me in awe. It sets my imagination into a roller-coaster ride of exploring what the possibilities could be.

As I sat reading chapter twenty-one of Revelation, it was with a sense of relief that I was able to read about a place of beauty. One gets a bit tired of reading twenty chapters of ugliness. This chapter is a vision Yeshua shows John of what the new Jerusalem looks like, the Jerusalem in spirit. This is not about a new Jerusalem on Earth. This is a glimpse into heaven. If John was expecting it to be an earthly place he would be disappointed. Whilst writing the last half of this book, Israel has been at war with the Palestinian people. The awful destruction of Palestine and Israel; the many people who have died or been left homeless because of political greed and the hunger to dominate; and the ugliness of ego driven power, is a long way off the vision John was seeing of this new Jerusalem. Remember – an eye for an eye leaves both people blind. And these political heads are sure blind to compassion, acceptance, and love.

I was intrigued to see, in verses eighteen to twenty-one, the amazing lineup of gem stones John saw in this new Jerusalem. For those who see the use of crystals as being 'new age-y', take a look at this little list of beauties:

18 *"And the building of the wall of it was of jasper [diamond]; and the city was pure gold, like unto clear glass."*

19 *"And the foundations of the wall of the city were garnished with all manner of precious stones. The first foundation was jasper [diamond]; the second sapphire; the third a chalcedony; the fourth, an emerald;"*

20 *"The fifth, sardonyx; the sixth, sardius [known now as carnelian]; the seventh, chrysolite; the eighth, beryl; the nineth, a topaz; the tenth, a chrysoprasus [chrysoprase]; the eleventh, a jacinth [zircon]."*

21 *"And the twelve gates were twelve pearls, every several gate was of one pearl; and the street of the city was pure gold, as it were transparent glass."*

If you have an interest in understanding the qualities of these stones, and the energy they transmit, there are plenty of sites, which will give you a deeper understanding as to why Yeshua chose these particular precious stones as the structure for the new Jerusalem or heaven. In his training as a young man in the art of crystal use, he knew exactly what each crystal represented. Two thousand years ago and beyond, the study and use of crystals was a common part of many cultures. There is nothing 'new age-y' about crystals. We are simply returning to a knowledge we once lost.

In verse twenty-two, John writes:

And I saw no temple therein; for the Lord God Almighty and the Lamb are the temple of it.

Lord God Almighty/ Great Spirit, is the energy of all that is of love and purity. The temple within heaven is not a physical structure, but the pure energy of love; and Yeshua, who embodies the Christ energy and is one of the greatest healers to have walked this planet, is the temple of love. And, as Yeshua was educated in his life here on Earth on the meaning of unconditional love, so too are we. Every person who lives and breathes on this journey with Earth are here to learn three major lessons:

- How to love unconditionally others and self.
- How to create a joyful and fulfilling life.
- How to be of service to others and the planet on which we are privileged to live.

We don't have to wait until we die to enter the new Jerusalem. We can create that sacred place within us right now. We start by flipping the coin, using alchemy to turn the negative into the positive. It all begins by loving the self!

We are all part of one immense energy field. What you do, not only has an impact on you, but it also has an impact on everyone else. When you walk with love as your number one priority – John says in verse twenty-six:

"And they shall bring the glory and honour of the nations into it."

Said differently, you will touch the lives of many and help our troubled world to heal.

27

THE RETURN OF YESHUA

The dawn of a new day, a new beginning.

We come to the last chapter of the book of Revelation, and in the first two verses John has a wonderful vision:

1 *"And he shewed me a pure river of water of life, clear as crystal, proceeding out of the throne of God and of the Lamb."*

2 *"In the midst of the street of it, and on either side of the river, was there the tree of life; which bare twelve manner of fruits, and yielded her fruit every month; and the leaves of the tree were for the healing of the nations."*

Remembering that the throne was not a physical structure but the seat or place of power. So, when John talks about the river that carries the water of life out of the throne, he is not talking about a physical river or a gilded chair. My understanding of what it means is this; from the place of divine power, that is both within us and within spirit, flows the energy of pure love. Being crystal clear means that such love is truly unconditional. It is that love which nurtures and nourishes us.

On either side of the river of love grows the tree of life. The symbol of the tree of life is quite popular in this modern age. You see it in jewelry, designed into suncatchers that hang on windows, used as a symbol for healing businesses, and often used in meditations. The majority of people who use the symbol are probably unaware that the origin of this symbol goes back two thousand years, and is mentioned in the last chapter of the last book of the Bible.

To use the metaphor:

The tree of life (us), draws from the pure crystal water of the river (the unconditional love of Great Spirit and Yeshua). And in doing so, we grow into our greatness, sending out our branches to all, and we flourish, yielding fruit (our gifts and wisdom), continuously. Within our leaves (our presence within the world), we carry the energy to heal self and all other people. In other words, the tree of life is a metaphor for our inner growth and expansion of our soul or spirit, how it can flourish when fed by the waters of divine love, and how it can be of service to humanity.

The twelve different fruits are a reference to the twelve tribes of Israel, as are the twelve gates in the previous chapter. We have, of course, since moved way beyond the confines of the Jewish tribes and the known world of that time.

As with all great masters of any religion, once back in spirit, religion holds no sway. Yeshua is present for all people regardless of what religious belief they carry here in their earthly life. There is no such thing as religion back in spirit. There is only the river of love flowing out from that seat of power – divine love.

In verse five we have reference to heaven (the new Jerusalem), having no negativity, no darkness, and that life is eternal.

5 "And there shall be no night there; and they need no candle, neither light of the sun; for the Lord God giveth them light; and they shall reign for ever and ever."

In verse seven Yeshua makes the statement – *"Behold I come quickly."* For two thousand years people have been waiting for his return. That does not feel so quick to me. Yeshua was not talking about a physical return. He was talking about returning to the people of Earth through spirit. Once he had done what he needed to do back in spirit, including bringing these visions to John, Yeshua did return quickly to help humanity, through his presence as a spirit being. As I debated with my dad, Yeshua is already back and has been for a very long time. I work with him on a daily basis, not as a Christian but soul to soul, spirit to spirit; working with him as the beautiful and wise Master he is, alongside the many other beautiful and wise masters who have walked this planet.

In verse nine, Yeshua again reprimands John for wanting to bow before him.

9 "Then saith he unto me, See thou do it not; for I am thy fellowservant."

It has never been Yeshua's intention for us to bow before him and place him on the pedestal. He wants us to understand the greatness we all carry inside of us; not the ego driven hunger for power kind of greatness, but the greatness of our soul and its capacity to love and be a healer, a magical creative being, one of wisdom in service to all. He wants to walk beside us as a dear friend and helper.

In verse sixteen, Yeshua says to John:

16. "I Jesus have sent mine angel to testify unto you these things in the churches. I am the root and offspring of David, and the bright and morning star."

Yeshua was born a prince in the line of King David. I think it was important for Yeshua to make that statement for it says two things:

- "I am a man of substance so these visions I have brought to you come from a soul who is well trained, and who knows what he is doing. They come from a leader."
- "Even the greatest are here to be of service to others; to help people find their way out of darkness back into the light."

And why the morning star rather than any other star? My home is called Balamara. It is an aboriginal word meaning 'morning star'. What do morning stars do? They guide people out of the dark night into the dawn of a new day, a new beginning.

And that, my dear reader, sums up the message in this entire book, and sums up who Yeshua truly is:

He is the morning star guiding people out of darkness into a new day. And so it is!

AFTERWORD

Writing this book has helped to heal the relationship with my dad and overcome the divide created through our differing perceptions of religion, and its role in our lives.

Today, as a medium, when I check in with my dad, rather than the stern eyes of concern for his wayward child, I see softness, laughter, acceptance, and – love!

And so it is, and so it will always be.

Amen!

PRAISE FOR JOY BRISBANE

READERS COMMENTS

Lauren Dean – Admissions Officer, St John of God Hospital, Ballarat

I am thoroughly enjoying reading Illumination. I love how open Joy is for the reader. She doesn't direct them on what to believe, but encourages an open mind, as she illuminates a new and deeper perspective behind these ancient writings.

I really loved the inclusions of the original passages from The Revelation, as I have not read it myself. I enjoyed the "flip" I felt after reading the original quotes. When I read them, I initially felt the uncomfortable squirm of feeling preached at. But upon reading Joy's deeper interpretations behind the words, it sparked a sense of relief and intrigue, as though the austere seriousness behind the original words suddenly melted away into something new and beautiful. Something that finally felt real and relatable to me. I felt the joy of discovery, surprise, and wonder, as though I was witnessing an ancient mystery unfolding and finally being solved.

Jan Smith – Owner and practitioner of alternate therapy healing centre – The Holistic Healing Tree

I really enjoyed reading Illumination.

I am finding - like *Creating Heaven on Earth* - that I am getting a better connection with Jesus. I work with him every day. He is my main guide with whom I work to help people heal. Reading this new book, I am finding that my healings have become more powerful, as they did when I read *Creating Heaven on Earth*. The way Joy explains how Jesus works in spirit, helps me to reconnect with him with a stronger energy.

I love reading Joy's books because they are so easy to understand, and without complication. They change my life by turning on another light bulb moment. Thanking you Joy, for just being you.

Allan Meers – Chartered Accountant

In her latest book, Illumination, Joy Brisbane takes us back to a time when visions and prophecies told of a new world order. The visions described in the Biblical Book of The Revelation describe dramatic events that have both terrified and perplexed me – until now.

Joy's perspective provides a fresh insight into the meaning behind the symbolic language used in The Revelation. She demystifies the images described by John almost 2,000 years ago and frames them within the context of the inner spiritual journey and the Roman occupation of the times. Joy's book gives me a reason to revisit the Bible and see its messages through new eyes – as someone who has discovered the gems hidden within an ancient scripture.

ALSO BY JOY BRISBANE

From the Contemporary Interpretations of Scripture Series Joy Brisbane bring us...

Creating Heaven on Earth - The Journey to Peace, Love and Happiness

NOTES

www.ingramcontent.com/pod-product-compliance
Lightning Source LLC
Chambersburg PA
CBHW062038290426
44109CB00026B/2661